Sunderland - a breath of fresh ai

Sunderland is a city with a difference – a modern, bustling centre that is balanced with a relaxing, green environment, stunning coastal scenery and a refreshing attitude to life.

Whether you're after relaxation, invigoration or both, Sunderland's distinctive mix of the city, coast and countryside will definitely be a breath of fresh air.

Attractions:
- Washington Wetland Centre
- Rainton Meadows Nature Reserve
- Roker and Seaburn beache
- Sunderland Museum & Winter Gardens
- National Glass Centre
- Northern Gallery for Contemporary Art
- Stadium of Light
- Penshaw Monument
- Washington Old Hall

C2C
&
REIVERS
TRAIL

THE COMPLETE CYCLE GUIDE

13th Edition

By Mark Porter

Accommodation, Food and Drink

History, Route and Maps

In the

Lake District, Pennines and Scottish Borders

C2C & Reivers Cycle Routes

13th Edition

By Mark Porter

**Accommodation, Food and Drink
History, Route and Maps
In the
Lake District, Pennines and Scottish Borders**

**By: Mark Porter
Design: Lewis Stuart
Copyright: Baytree Press ©**

**Published by:
Baytree Press,
Bridge Street, Rothbury,
Northumberland NE65 7SG**

✆ +44 (0) 7767 893790
📠 info@c2c-guide.co.uk
💻 www.c2c-accommodation.co.uk

ISBN 978-0-9555082-2-6

**Cordee Books & Maps
3a de Montfort Street,
Leicester LE1 7HD**

✆ +44 1162 543579
📠 Sales@cordee.co.uk
💻 www.cordee.co.uk

Contents

Before you start

Introduction

This year is the 14th anniversary of Britain's most popular and best known cycle route. It is also the 14th anniversary of this publication and website. The revamped pocket guide should give you better than ever information in a user-friendly format.

The website (www.c2caccommodation.co.uk), as you may notice, is also being beefed up, with extra content. We have also taken over www.c2c-guide.co.uk to give riders and advertisers an even wider spread of information and also have started selling commemorative T-shirts and Sustrans maps covering a variety of routes on the www.c2c-guide.co.uk site.

There is something about propelling oneself from one side of Britain to the other which captures the imagination. It is an easily quantifiable achievement – just like Land's End to John O'Groats, but on a much more manageable scale. It combines the majestic beauty of the Northern Lakes, whose unspoilt charms are much the same as they would have been in Wordsworth's day, with the beauty of the Eden Valley, and the challenge of the Pennines.

Then the route crosses areas of post-industrial heritage before entering Newcastle and Sunderland. This epic journey has everything you could want on a route which holds appeal to expert and beginner alike, and can be managed over a long weekend.

The route was set up by the cycling charity Sustrans and this guide is designed to be used with the C2C Sustrans Map obtainable from the National Cycle Network Centre (aka Sustrans).

National Cycle Network Centre,
Cathedral Square, College Green, Bristol BS1 5DD

☎ +44 (0)845 113 0065

For speed:

PO Box 21, Bristol BS99 2HA

You can also get it from tourist information centres or via the website

🖳 www.sustrans.org.uk

Reivers

As for the Reivers Route, which will take you back to your starting point via some spectacular and remote countryside, this is available from Footprint, who have kindly allowed us to reproduce some of their mapping plus map profiles which allow you to access the hilly bits.

Unit 87,
Stirling Enterprise Park,
Stirling, FK7 7RP
+44 (0)1786 479886
www.footprintmaps.co.uk.

Your hosts have been chosen for their understanding of the cyclist's needs, a warm welcome, acceptance of muddy legs, a secure place for your bike and provision of a meal either with them or at a nearby pub.

The C2C is designed to be tackled west to east to take advantage of the prevailing winds. Both the Sustrans map and this accommodation guide run from west to east, while the return leg along the Reivers
– for those brave
enough to tackle
the whole circuit
– was tailor-made
for an east-west crossing of the UK.

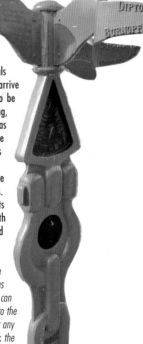

Please try to book accommodation, meals and packed lunches in advance, and do not arrive unannounced expecting beds and meals to be available. If you have to cancel a booking, please give the proprietor as much notice as you can so that the accommodation can be re-let. Your deposit may be forfeited: this is at the discretion of the proprietor.

Suggestions for additional addresses are most welcome, together with your comments. We are particularly keen to receive reports about the efficacy of waymarking on both routes, and comments (both positive and adverse) on our route tips and guidance.

● *Please note that the information given in the guide was correct at the time of printing and was as supplied by the proprietors. No responsibility can be accepted by this independent company as to the completeness or accuracy of all entries, nor for any loss arising as a result. It is advisable to check the relevant details when booking.*

Foreword

*T*he C2C ride has been a memorable experience for more than 150,000 cyclists over the last 14 years – an achievable challenge, a memorable ride, wonderful scenery, and so often excellent hospitality along the way. When you arrive wet and exhausted, nothing matters quite so much as the welcome you receive, a place to put your bike, somewhere to dry your clothes and

a hot bath. Somehow these routines of everyday life become so much more important on a journey like the C2C.

This guide can help you find just this welcome, so that staying overnight along the route is just as memorable as the journey itself. At the same time, your expenditure is supporting the local economy with more than £15 million spent so far, spread out over the length of the route.

By cycling you do more than support just local businesses, you demonstrate that the tourist industry can touch lightly on the beautiful countryside we all flock to see; that it isn't necessary to drive for this pleasure; and that you have made your own personal contribution towards a sustainable future for the stressed-out planet we all share.

I hope that inspired by this trip you will cycle more – there is the whole 10,000 miles of the National Cycle Network to start with.

John Grimshaw
Founder SUSTRANS

The route

The C2C is designed to be cycled from west coast to east coast. This is because of prevailing winds and gradients: do it this way and, god-willing, the wind will be behind you and most of the climbs will be short and sharp, rather than long and grinding. East to west, therefore, is for those who like unrelentingly hostile gradients with the wind in their face. If you want to cycle east to west, a more user-friendly route is the Reivers (see page 101)

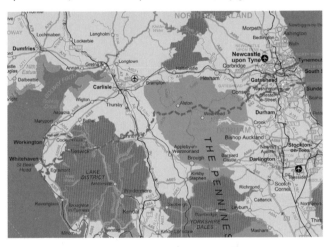

Acknowledgements

As ever, many thanks to David Gray, the Sustrans man who was instrumental in putting together the C2C, along with John Grimshaw and the late John Naylor. Some of their images have been reproduced in the following pages, along with those of Martin Herron, Julia Bayne, Barry Wilson, Pat Strachan, G.L. Jones and Steve Morgan.

Thanks also to Newcastle Gateshead Initiative, the Cumbria Tourist Board picture library and Ben Barden, Footprint Maps for their co-operation with the splendid Reivers route, and www.thecumbriadirectory.com, whose excellent website provided useful background information.

SUSTRANS stands for sustainable transport. It is a government sponsored charity which is in the process of turning many of Britain's minor byways and pathways into a national network of cycle routes as part of a crusade to encourage us to use the combustion engine less. It has transformed 10,000 miles of old road, track and pathway into the National Cycle Network, of which the C2C is a small but important part. If you would like to become a member of Sustrans you can do so by writing to them.

No chance of missing the Whitehaven starting point thanks to this Chris Bramhall designed marker.
Picture: John Grimshaw/ Sustrans

Getting there

TRAIN

There are three choices of start, and two choices of finish. All three possible starts, Whitehaven, Workington and Egremont & St Bees are accessible by train on the local First North Western line from Carlisle. The journey follows the spectacular, dramatic coastline and takes about an hour. Remember to book your bike on in advance.

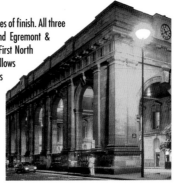

There is a cross country service to Carlisle, where you pick up the connection to the starting point of choice. I have heard reports of the rail services being unhelpful to cyclists but I gather there has been a big change in attitude and they are now altogether more helpful – though this is at the discretion of the guard or ticket inspector.

National Rail Enquiries:
☎08457 484950
First North Western:
☎08457 000125 (sales)

Virgin Trains (West Coast):
☎08457 222333
There are excellent services to get you home direct from Newcastle Central Station, *pictured*.
Direct line: ☎ +44 (0)191 221 3156
National Express: ☎ +44 (0)8457 225225

Sunderland Station
● There is a ban on taking bicycles on the Tyne and Wear Metro, but they are carried by the other train operators from Sunderland Station.
● It's on the regional link between Newcastle and Middlesbrough/Darlington.
● Cyclists are welcome on Grand Central trains from London to Sunderland via the Durham Heritage Coast and York.

AIR

Newcastle Airport is only 20 minutes from the city centre and there are regular and frequent links to many major European cities, including Amsterdam, Brussels and Paris, along with international connections to the rest of the world. Within the UK, there are also direct flights to Aberdeen, Birmingham, Gatwick, Heathrow, Wick, Dublin and Belfast.
☎ + 44 (0)191 286 0966
🖥 www.newcastleairport.com

SEA

The International Ferry Terminal at Royal Quays is the North of England's main sea link with Scandinavia and Continental Europe with regular passenger services from Norway, Sweden and the Netherlands. It is an ideal start point for the Reivers, Hadrian's Wall or C2C in reverse if you don't fancy geting the train across to Whitehaven, Workington or St Bees & Egremont.
DFDS Seaways
☎+44 (0)191 293 6262

Motorised alternatives, in the form of specialist taxi services, are readily available for the return journey. Some of them will organise the whole package for you.

The Bike Bus, Stanley Mini Coaches, Stanley
☎ 01207 237424 (see Back Cover)

Tyne Valley Holidays, Newcastle
☎ 0191 284 7534 (See Page 141)

Cycle Active, Langwathby
☎ 01768 881111

CAR

All three starting points are easily accessible by road.

From the south and east: Take the M6 to Penrith, where you pick up the A66 through Keswick to your chosen starting point. The road goes straight into Workington, or turn onto the A595 at Bridgefoot for Whitehaven or Egremont.

From the north: Head to Carlisle, leaving the city on the A595. For Workington, turn onto the A596 at Thursby. Stick with the road you are on for Whitehaven or Egremont.

Most accommodation owners will allow you to leave your vehicle with them. Or you may prefer a secure long-term car park. There is one in the centre of Whitehaven.

There is £3-a-day parking one mile from the start of the C2C at one of the last mile points on the home leg of the Reivers Route, run by a Sustrans ranger, no less.
Contact Jim Hewitson
☎ +44 (0)1946 692178

In Workington, there's parking at the quayside for £2.50 a day:
Contact Martin Perkins
☎ +44 (0)1900 604997

For further information call the Tourist Information Centre:
Whitehaven ☎ +44 (0)1946 852939
Workington ☎ +44 (0)1900 606699
Back-up vehicles are kindly requested to use main roads in order to keep the C2C route as traffic-free as possible.

WAY MARKING

The route is waymarked with a blue direction sign complete with the letters C2C and a red number 7 – the number of the route. These are posted at junctions and other strategic spots. Occasionally the road surface is signed; sometimes there are just little plastic stickers posted to gates and

lamp-posts. Signage is not always brilliant, but with sharp eyes and the use of a map you should not get lost. Having said that, sections at the beginning and end are notorious for the lack of signs; vandals like to trash them and souvenir hunters snaffle them.

MAPS

There is basic mapping in this guide, along with topographical maps showing profiles of such beastly climbs as Hartside. You will also need the Sustrans C2C map. If you want to, take the Ordnance Survey maps but they are bulky and the waymarking means they are unnecessary. You could also invest in the OS Interactive Atlas, and download or print the relevant sections. The two-CD option costs around £30.

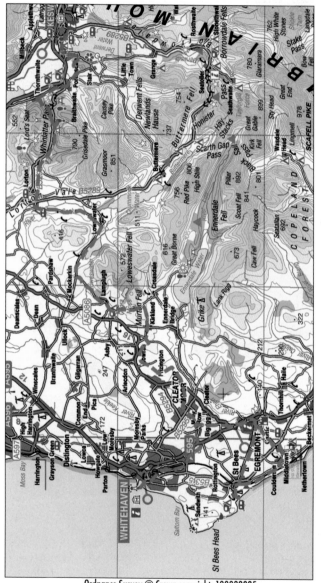

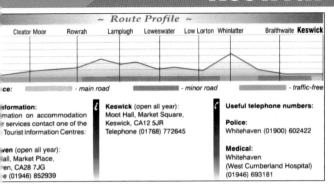

~ Route Profile ~

Cleator Moor · Rowrah · Lamplugh · Loweswater · Low Lorton · Whinlatter · Braithwaite **Keswick**

ce: ▓▓▓▓ - main road ▓▓▓▓ - minor road ▓▓▓▓ - traffic-free

information:
mation on accommodation
r services contact one of the
Tourist Information Centres:

ven (open all year):
all, Market Place,
en, CA28 7JG
e (01946) 852939

Keswick (open all year):
Moot Hall, Market Square,
Keswick, CA12 5JR
Telephone (01768) 772645

Useful telephone numbers:

Police:
Whitehaven (01900) 602422

Medical:
Whitehaven
(West Cumberland Hospital)
(01946) 693181

Whitehaven

DEPARTURE ROUTE

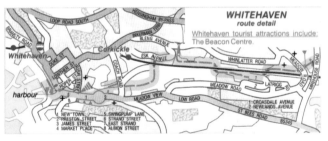

WHITEHAVEN
route detail
Whitehaven tourist attractions include:
The Beacon Centre.

1 NEW TOWN 5 SWINGPUMP LANE
2 PRESTON STREET 6 STRAND STREET
3 JAMES STREET 7 EAST STRAND
4 MARKET PLACE 8 ALBION STREET

1 CROASDALE AVENUE
2 NEWLANDS AVENUE

Harbour to the edge of town

As you leave Whitehaven harbour you will join the Whitehaven-Rowrah cycle path, which links the sea to the fells.

First, detailed instructions for getting onto the route proper:

🚲 Out of the harbour head right up Quay Street.

🚲 Left past the Tourist Information Centre through Market Place and into Preston Street. Look out for signs on the left for the path behind Focus DIY.

🚲 Onto Esk Avenue, only to rejoin the path by the school. You then cycle along Croasdale Avenue and Wasdale Avenue before linking up with the path to exit the town.

You now follow the railway line built in the 1850s to carry limestone, coal and iron; it is now a sculpture trail interpreting the geology and industrial history of the region. You might find yourself stopping to check signage; this is routine, there are several other routes around here including the Egremont link.

13

ABOUT THE TOWN

Whitehaven has the distinction of being both the starting point of the C2C and the finish for the Reivers Cycle Route. It may not be quite the place it was in the 18th century, when it played a significant role in the British slave industry and was the main importer of tobacco on the west coast, but it has undergone a major transformation in the last couple of years and its fine Georgian architecture is now looking spruce and proud again.

Perhaps the most impressive feature is the large harbour, which has undergone a £68 million facelift. There is a fine 100-berth marina, now choc-a-bloc with pleasure craft of all sizes and shapes. The town has, in short, re-acquired some of the prosperity it lost in the years after it became the world's first new town.

Not so long ago it would have been hard to imagine that early Manhattan's street grid system was based on the pattern the Lowther family laid out for Whitehaven in the late 1690s, when it became apparent that the Cumbrian settlement was destined for great things.

Shortly afterwards the streets filled with rum and sugar merchants, slave traders and tobacco speculators as well as America-bound settlers waiting for their boat to come and take them off to a new life in the New World. The harbour was teeming with coal transporters, which plied the Irish Sea to supply Dublin's houses and industries with black stuff dynamited from under Whitehaven's seabed.

There was also shipbuilding; more than 1,000 vessels were built in the Whitehaven yards, and one of the oldest surviving iron-built ships was constructed here. After London and Bristol, this was the busiest port in England.

PLACES OF INTEREST

The Beacon
Local maritime and industrial history within the Harbour Gallery and magnificent views over the town. Done up during 2007.
☎ 01946 592302

Michael Moon's, Bookshop & Gallery
Roper Street
One of the largest bookshops in Cumbria, "vast and gloriously eccentric!"

The Rum Story
Exhibition celebrating the Jefferson family business, the oldest booze empire in Britain.

The Haig Mining Museum
Haig Enterprise Park, High Road
Memories of the last deep pit in Cumbria.

AMERICAN LINKS

Whitehaven's connections with America go deep: John Paul Jones, founder of the American navy and erstwhile scourge of Britain's own, gained his sea legs as a merchant seaman from Whitehaven.

Indeed, the last invasion of the English mainland, in 1778, was perpetrated by Jones upon the town. The incursion was part of the only attack on British soil by US forces; and we should not forget that George Washington's granny, Mildred Warner Gale, lived here and is buried at St Nicholas's churchyard.

The town has been impressively preserved, one suspects, because a sudden lack of prosperity after the boom years disinclined planners from bulldozing in the name of progress. This left the Lowther architectural heritage preserved, as it were, in aspic. It is worthwhile walking the streets, admiring this memorial to an earlier and prosperous age, when sea captains and merchants lived in style.

There are many interesting and quirky sculptures around the harbour, a number of street mosaics featuring different aspects of the town's heritage, plus a mural in Washington Square and a plethora of shiny plaques above doorways giving clues to the past.

It is one of my favourite places on the whole route and it seems a shame just to use Whitehaven as a point of departure without spending the previous night exploring. There are plenty of distractions, in the form of pubs, restaurants and venues. The following day's ride out of this port is nothing if not leisurely - a stark contrast to the undulations that are to follow. A late night is not going to spoil it.

The traditional way to start this route is by christening your bike on the slipway behind the big C2C sign by dipping the front wheel in the briny. Then you might wish to get your first route stamp at the New Espresso café in the Market Place.

WHERE TO EAT

The Lime Lounge
9 Marlborough Street
℘ 0871 5297853

Georgian House
Church Street
℘ 01946 696611

Casa Romana [Italian]
Queen Street
℘ 01946 591901

Jasmine Palace [Chinese/Thai]
Duke/Strand Street
℘ 0871 5297754

Blue Wine Bar & Restaurant
Tangier Street
℘ 01946 691986

Westminster Restaurant
Lowther Street
℘ 01946 694404

Askash Tandoori [Indian]
℘ 01946 691171

Ali Taj Restaurant [Indian]
34/35 Tangier St
℘ 01946 592679

China Palace [Chinese]
George Street
℘ 01946 693388

Zest Harbourside
℘ 01946 66981

Howgate Brewster & Travel Inn
℘ 01946 66286

Waverley Hotel

Tangier St, CA28 7UX
Run by: Cheryl Twinn

Bustling privately owned town centre hotel, traditional in style, licensed and with busy restaurant. Close to harbour and popular amongst cyclists.

- ☎ 01946 694337
- 🖥 www.thewaverleyhotel.co.uk
- ✉ thewaverleyhotel@hotmail.com
- 🛏 10S, 5D,6T,3F
- 💰 £28-£50S; £52-£64D
- 🍽 Eve Meal: £5.95-£15
- 🍽 Pk Lunch: from £4.95
- 🍸 Fully Licensed
- 🚴 Dist to C2C: On route

The Mansion

Old Woodhouse, Whitehaven, Cumbria CA28 9LN
Run by: Tom Todd & Philip Kirkbride

Friendly, relaxed and with all mod cons. Super big screen TV and swimming pool opening this year.

- ☎ 01946 61860
- ☎ 01946 691270
- ✉ comnenus4@aol.com
- 🛏 12 rooms
- 💰 From £20–£25
- 🍽 Pk Lunch: £3.50
- 🍽 Eve Meal: £6.00-£10
- 🍸 Nr pub: 100m
- 🚴 Dist to C2C: 1 Km

Glenfield Guest House

Whitehaven, Cumbria, CA28 7TS
Run by: Margaret & Andrew Davies

Set in a conservation area close to the town centre but with a home-from-home atmosphere. Specialises in home cooking and luxury en-suite accommodation. Licensed lounge with open fire. Free WiFi and on-line booking.

- ☎ 01946 691911
- 🖥 www.glenfield-whitehaven.co.uk
- ✉ glenfieldGH@aol.com
- 🛏 1S, 2D, 1T, 2F
- 💰 £27.50-£55
- 🍽 Eve Meal: £4.50-£8.50
- 🍽 Pk Lunch: £4.50
- 🍸 Nr pub: 50m
- 🚴 Dist to C2C: 400m
- ⓘ AA 4-star. Welcome to Excellence Award. Food Safety Performance—4 stars

St Bees & Egremont

BY popular request we decided last year to introduce a third possible start to the route: St Bees, the seaside neighbour of the newly vibrant Egremont.

St Bees is the tried and trusted start to the Coast to Coast walk, famously founded by Alfred Wainwright in 1973. It is also a lovely coastal setting and a splendid but smaller alternative to the bustling charms of Whitehaven and Workington.

The Egremont area has been mining iron ore and quarrying for more than 800 years and it is home to Florence Mine, the last deep Iron Ore mine in Western Europe.

There is plenty of eager and competitive accommodation in Egremont, plus numerous hostelries and eateries in the area. Indeed, huge efforts are being put into the regeneration of this former weaving and dyeing town.

Egremont's hidden gems include the Norman Castle with its literary connection to Wordsworth's Ballad of the Horn of Egremont; Hartley's ice cream factory and shop; Lowes Court Gallery and its Tourist Information Centre (℘01946 820693) with exhibitions of Cumbrian artists and local crafts.

As a 'Fairtrade Town' Egremont has a number of shops selling locally produced and sourced foods and holds a Farmers Market on the third Friday of every month in the Market Hall.The main street has a variety of facilities, shops, pubs and takeaways catering for visitor needs.

During the annual Crab Fair, which celebrated its 840th anniversary in September 2007, the greasy pole climbing and gurning (face pulling) events draw large crowds of locals and visitors. Indeed, the town is synonymous with that time honoured English tradition of gurning.

This year will see further improvements to the town and its facilities, such as circular cycling routes, riverside walks and new planting to the town's entrances as part of the Egremont Market Town Initiative work. The Tourist Information Centre at Lowes Court Gallery is always there for details of things to do in and around the town.

℘ 01946 820693

The local regeneration partnership is keen to improve the visitor offer further and welcomes your comments, suggestions and information by email, through its website or by post:

regeneration@VisitEgremont.co.uk

www.VisitEgremont.co.uk

Egremont & Area Regeneration Partnership, Charles Edmonds Library, Wyndam Street, Egremont, CA22 2DH

DIRECTIONS

St Bees to merge point with Whitehaven route

Those arriving at St Bees by train should leave the station to the Priory Church side and make their way along the 'Coach Road' past the petrol station and garage to the beach.

St Bees Head is the most westerly point in the North of England and on a clear day from the promenade you can look out to the Isle of Man, 20 miles or so off the coast.

The first stage of the route takes you to Egremont, four miles away.

Leave the beach car park and take the first right along the straight road to the Station. Cross the level crossing and continue up the Main Street past the Platform 9 restaurant and the Queens Hotel on your right, the Manor House Hotel and the post office on your left.

At the next junction you have the choice to take:

🚲 The challenging route left up Outrigg (20%) and over Baybarrow, with rewarding views over to Ennerdale, Wasdale and down the coast to Eskdale and further

🚲 Continue up the Main Street to take the second right – signposted for the Hadrians Way C72 route – and follow the coast (Nethertown Road) and charming single-track lanes to Coulderton, then head inland for Egremont and the Lakes.

At the T-junction in Coulderton, head right to Middletown, taking first left just before the telephone box. Follow the lane for a short while, but instead of heading right, go straight on past Black Ling and Pickett How, up the narrow minor road. Make sure to enjoy views across to Dent Fell – the western edge of the Lake District as you head towards Egremont. Arriving in Egremont, take time to visit the Castle (pictured), then follow the national cycle route 72 which is clearly signed through the town and out to the north.

About a mile north of Egremont is Clintz Quarry Nature Reserve, a limestone quarry of dramatic proportions with 100ft cliffs. It is home to some rare orchids in May and June, and is a sanctuary for birds.

Shepherds Arms Hotel
Ennerdale Bridge, Ennerale,
Cumbria, CA23 3AR
Run by: Malcolm Thomas-Chapman

A small gem of a country hotel with public bar serving real ales and pub meals. On the Coast to Coast walk and the increasingly popular new start to the C2C out of St Bees. A busy local pub with comfortable rooms.

- ☎ 01946 861249
- 🖥 www.shepherdsarmshotel.co.uk
- ✉ shepherdsarms@btconnect.com
- 🛏 3D, 3T, 2D/T
- 💰 £38.50-£48.50
- 🍽 Eve Meal: Under £10 for a main course
- 🍽 Pk Lunch: £3.95-£5.50

The Manor House Hotel Bar
11/12 Main St, CA27 0DE
Run by: Margaret Fee

Traditional ales (it's in the Good Beer Guide), comfortable, clean and with a great atmosphere (the mixture of locals and tourists in the bar works well). The dining room is also used as a cafe. This 18th century coaching inn welcomes cyclists and walkers and has a secure lock-up.

- ☎ 01946 822425
- 🖥 www.themanorhousestbees.com
- ✉ manorhousemaz@aol.com
- 🛏 1S, 4T, 3D, 1Q.
- 💰 £29-£35
- 🍽 Eve Meal: £4.95-£14.95
- 🍽 Pk Lunch: £5-£7

Egremont Cycle Barn
Horse & Groom Court, Egremont CA22 2AE
Run by: Rob Merrett

Right in the town centre. Opened in early

2008 and is available for bookings. It is self-catering but there are plenty of shops, pubs and restaurants nearby. There is a secure lock-up for bikes and cleaning facilities.

- ☎ 01946 824052
- 🖥 www.horseandgroomcourt.co.uk
- ✉ info@horseandgroomcourt.co.uk
- 🛏 1 six bed dorm, 1Q, 3T. All en-suite wet rooms
- 💰 £8
- 🍽 Self-catering or nearby pubs/restaurants

Bookwell Garth Guest House
16 Bookwell, Egremont, CA22 2LS
Run by: Wayne & Jeannette Powell

Friendly Guest House with good accommodation, TV in all rooms. Drying facilities, good location. Large upstairs lounge with fridge, microwave and tea and coffee. Early breakfast. Large car park.

- ☎ 01946 820271
- ✉ jeannette.powell@tesco.net

- 🛏 5S, 6T, 1F.
- 💰 £21-£26
- 🍺 Pub nearby
- 🚲 Dist to C2C: On route's new leg

Lorton

The River Lorton as you approach the villagew

DIRECTIONS
Merging of the routes to Lorton

Whether you have come up the disused railway line from Whitehaven or joined the main cycle route from Egremont, the next stage sees you cut through Cleator Moor and rejoin the old railway heading towards Rowrah and Kirkland.

Beyond Rowrah turn left onto the lane and right at the school. You will soon pass Felldyke where you follow the signs for Lamplugh and Loweswater.

In about 5km you will be skirting the Loweswater lake, your first glimpse of the Lakes and a wonderful spot to take pictures or stop for a snack. Beyond is the picturesque village of Loweswater, complete with church and village inn; a delightful place to stop if you are really taking your time, or are on foot.

Head left at Loweswater, up the lane through Thackthwaite and soon you will cross the River Cocker at Low Lorton, passing through Lorton Vale and into High Lorton. This is a truly picturesque Northern Lakes village to spend a night.

ON ARRIVAL

Alfred Wainwright, Britain's most famous walking hero and pioneer of the outdoors, regarded this area, with its deeply gouged valleys reached from the passes of Whinlatter, Honister and Newlands, as his favourite spot.

Lorton is only about 5km south of Cockermouth, so it is also an optional diversion for those who have decided to start their journey from Workington.

To get to New House (below) on the B5289:

🚴 Carry on straight through Loweswater for 3km on the road parallel with the route:

🚴 Turn right onto the B5289 at the crossroads just beyond the Lorton bridge. It's only 2km from the route.

New House Farm

Lorton, Cockermouth, Cumbria CA139UU
Run by: Hazel Thompson

Winning 17th century grade II listed farmhouse set in stunning surroundings, now boasting a tea room with declicious home-made produce. Beautiful antiques throughout compliment the original oak beams, flag floors and stone fireplaces where log fires crackle on colder days. Four posters, hot tub in the garden. Delicious food.

- 01900 85404
- 07841 159818
- www.newhouse-farm.com
- enquiries@newhouse-farm.co.uk
- 5D, 1T (E-S)
- £75
- Pk Lunch: £7.50
- Eve Meal: £24 for 3 courses
- Diversion from route: 2km
- VisitBritain 5 stars. Which? Hotel of the year award winner
- Pub 2km. Tea room now available

Meadow Bank

High Lorton, Cockermouth,
Cumbria CA13 9UG
Run by: Christine Edmunds

The reception here is as warm as the rooms and the location could hardly be bettered. Secure bike storage, drying facilities—pub close by and a great breakfast to see you on your way.

- 01900 85315
- www.MeadowBankbandb.co.uk
- CEdm85315@aol.com
- 1D,1T (E-S)
- £26—£28
- Pk Lunch: £4
- Dist to C2C: 300m
- Pub 1km

Winder Hall Country House

Low Lorton, Cockermouth, Cumbria CA13 9UP
Run by: Ann and Nick Lawler

Beautiful hide-away in a historic manor house just off C2C. A popular stopping point for sandwiches and coffee before the tough climb up Whinlatter. Also popular for afternoon teas and a good resting place for those who like to take things easy. Indeed, not a bad overnight for anyone coming back along the Reivers (about 3 miles south of the route down the B5292). The rooms are very pretty and the food is organic and excellent.

- 01900 85107
- 01900 85479
- www.winderhall.co.uk
- stay@winderhall.co.uk
- 7D, 2T, 2F, 2 Four-posters (E-S)
- £37-£64; £71-£101 (DB&B)
- Eve Meal: £26-£37
- Dist to C2C:100m
- 5 Diamonds. Fine Dining Award

Over Whinlatter

DIRECTIONS

The first real challenge comes when you leave High Lorton: the uphill slog to Whinlatter, the first section of which is unremitting, until you join the B5292 on the Whinlatter Pass.

You should bear right along the forest track, then first left along the wide track, ignoring other routes to the right. This takes you over rough terrain for a couple of kilometres before coming out on the B5292, at which point go left then right for the Whinlatter Visitor Centre (if for any reason the off-road track is closed, as it was when I last cycled the C2C, continue along the road to the visitor centre).

You are in the heart of England's only mountain forest. Because of the pure mountain air a sanatorium used to stand in the Whinlatter Forest. Sailors with TB and other communicable diseases were kept there in isolation. Beyond the visitor centre, pictured below, the route goes sharp right down a forest track to Thornthwaite, commanding some stunning views of Bassenthwaite Lake.

Take time, weather permitting, to admire Blencathra, Skiddaw and, over to the right, Helvellyn.

There is now an extensive range of mountain bike routes and Whinlatter is fast becoming the hub for northern Lakeland off-roading.

Also leave yourself enough time to have a good look around the visitor centre. A must for ornithologists, it also contains a wealth of forest habitat information and has a fine tea room.

After Thornthwaite the route links up with the Workington to Keswick alternative, via Braithwaite and Portinscale, where there are some charming accommodation possibilities.

● *The merged section starts on Page 33*

The view from Whinlatter

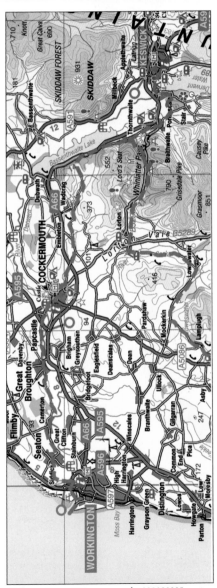

Ordnance Survey © Crown copyright: 100039985

Riding surface: ▬▬▬ - main road   ▬▬▬ - minor road   ▬▬▬ - traffic-fr

i Tourist Information:
For information on accommodation and other services contact one of the following Tourist Information Centres:

Cockermouth (open all year):
Town Hall, Market Street,
Cockermouth, CA13 9NP
Telephone (01900) 822634

i Whitehaven (open all year):
Market Hall, Market Place,
Whitehaven, CA28 7JG
Telephone (01946) 852939

✆ Useful telephone numbers:
Police:
Workington & Cockermouth
(01900) 602422
Medical:
Workington Infirmary
(01900) 602244
Cockermouth Doctors
(01900) 324100

Workington
DEPARTURE ROUTE

Workington heading for Cockermouth

The route starts from the lighthouse. You get there by turning down Curwen Road on the industrial estate. From the lighthouse turn left onto the railway bridge just by the sailing club, then (briefly) follow the path by the side of the river Derwent.

Bear left at the next railway bridge, crossing the line at the road junction, where you turn right.

At the main road go right and under the sandstone bridge where you meet the walkway/cycle path which then bears left, heading out of the industrial part of Workington past the lagoon and up through Seaton.

Follow the route through Camerton, briefly joining the river again, skirting Broughton Moor and on through

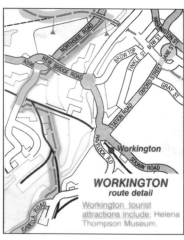

WORKINGTON
route detail

Workington tourist attractions include: Helena Thompson Museum.

Great Broughton and Papcastle, once the site of a Roman fort. You are now on the edge of Cockermouth.

ABOUT THE TOWN

Back from the brink

European funding is being used to help restore this fine working town and there are high hopes that its resurgence will bring with it tourism and a new lease of life, as has happened in Whitehaven and Maryport, further up the coast.

Work on the town centre has just finished, after two years of mayhem and now there are new shops and a fine new silver municipal clock. There are some splendid examples of Georgian architecture and some powerful industrial heritage.

Workington is an ancient market and industrial town at the mouth of the River Derwent.

Parts of it date back to Roman times but it was not until the 18th century, with the exploitation of local iron ore and coal that Workington expanded to become a major industrial town and port.

In this respect its growth mirrors that of its neighbour, Whitehaven, 12km down the coast. Iron and steel manufacturing have always been part of Workington's raison d'etre, and it was here that Henry Bessemer first introduced his revolutionary steel making process, florally commemorated in the picture below.

In recent years, with the decline of the steel industry and coal mining, the town has had to diversify and with the refurbishment of the town centre it is ready to welcome tourists to its heart.

The advantage of starting here is that the opening leg of the journey is 11km shorter, has gentler gradients and passes through the beautiful market town of Cockermouth.

It is also close to, and goes through, Camerton, where the church sits prettily on the banks of the Derwent and the splendidly named Black Tom Inn beckons alluringly to passers-by.

It has some nice churches. The parish church of St Michael's has been on its present site since the 7th century, although the 12th century Norman church was replaced in 1770 by a larger building. Sadly this was severely damaged by fire in 1994, but has since undergone a major rebuilding programme. St John's Church was built in 1823 to commemorate the battle of Waterloo, to a design by Thomas Hardwick. It is built of local sandstone, and bears some resemblance to Inigo Jones's St Paul's Church in Covent Garden, London.

(i) Workington Tourist Information Centre

(01900 606699

PLACES OF INTEREST

Workington Hall

Workington Hall is built around a pele tower dating from the 14th century, and was once one of the finest manor houses in the region.

This striking ruin, once owned by the Curwen family, Lords of the Manor of Workington, gave shelter to Mary Queen of Scots on her last flight from Scotland before her imprisonment and execution.

It is said to be haunted by Henry Curwen, who sunk the nearby Jane Pit in the 19th century, the remains of which can be seen at nearby Mossbay.

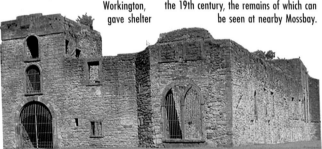

TOWN MUSEUM

The Helena Thompson Museum was bequeathed to the people of Workington by the eponymous Miss Thompson, a local philanthropist, in 1940. It houses displays of pottery, silver, glass, and furniture dating from Georgian times, as well as the social and industrial history of Workington and the surrounding area.

WHERE TO EAT

Impressions,
173 Vulcans Lane
Traditional English food
✆ 01900 605 446

Super Fish
20 Pow Street
Sit-in or takeaway
✆ 01900 604 916

Blue Dolphin
1 Lismore Place
Sit-in or t-away
✆ 01900 604114

Carnegie Colours Cafe
Finkle Street
Home-cooking
✆ 01900 605743

Treats
26 Finkle Street
Good cafe
✆ 01900 871752

The Old Townhouse
Portland Square
Upmarket
✆ 01900 871332

Tarantella
15-19 Wilson Street
Good new Italian
✆ 0871 5297487.

CYCLE SHOPS

Bike Bank
18-20 Market Place
✆ 01900 603 337

Halfords
Derwent Howe Retail Park
✆ 01900 601635

Morven House Hotel

Siddick Road, Workington, Cumbria CA14 1LE
Run by: Mrs Caroline Nelson

"A relaxed, informal atmosphere, an ideal stopover for C2C /Reivers participants near start. Car park and secure cycle storage."

- 01900 602118
- www.morvenguesthouse.com
- cnelsonmorven@aol.com
- 2D, 6T
- £28-£34
- Pk Lunch: £4.50
- Eve Meal: £10-£12
- Distance from C2C: On route
- VisitBritain 3 stars
- Pub nearby

Armidale Cottages

29 High Seaton, CA14 1PD
Run by: Susan and Fred Dahl

Just a few hundred yards from the track and five minutes from the start/finish, Armidale is set in half an acre of land with a small orchard. It has wood-burning stoves in the lounge and dining room and is centrally heated. There are slate floors in the lounge and hall with wood floors in the dining room and bedroom. Great breakfast and top end accommodation. Credit cards now accepted. Also handy for the Hadrian Way.

- 01900 63704
- www.armidalecottages.co.uk
- armidalecotts@hotmail.com
- 2D
- £28-£35
- Nr pub: The Coachman, 5 minutes walk
- Pk Lunch: On request
- Local inspection: Commended

The River Cocker is an ever-present landmark

Cockermouth

This is one of the most attractive towns in the northwest and is one of only two places in the Lake District to be designated a 'Gem Town' by the Department of the Environment 40 years ago. That means it is protected and will, in essence, remain the same in perpetuity.

It is just outside the boundary of the Lake District National Park and perhaps for this reason is not inundated with tourists and the tackiness that often goes with the industry.

It developed at the confluence of two great salmon rivers – the Cocker, which flows out of lakes Buttermere, Crummock and Loweswater; and the Derwent, which runs through lakes Derwent and Bassenthwaite to Workington.

The town got its market charter in 1221, and has retained its importance over the centuries. Later there was quarrying and mining for lead and iron outside the town, and a brewery at the foot of the castle mound, where the two rivers meet.

It has long fascinated writers, poets and artists and is the birthplace of William and Dorothy Wordsworth – one of the finest buildings here is Wordsworth House, pictured, the Lakeland poet's family home, which is now in the care of the National Trust.

The great architectural guru Sir Nikolaus Pevsner in his `Buildings of England', described the place as `quite a swagger house for such a town'. Built in 1745 for the then High Sheriff of Cumberland, Joshua Lucock, it was bought in 1761 by Sir James Lowther, son of Sir John, who built Whitehaven and its port.

John Wordsworth, the poet's father, moved to Cockermouth as agent to Sir James in 1764, and in 1766 married and moved into the house. Here four sons and a daughter were born. Their mother died when William was eight, and he went to live with relations in Penrith.

The house thrived as a private residence until 1937, when it was put on the market. Since it was in a prime location in the centre of town, bosses of the local bus company snapped it up as the natural spot for a bus station. They applied for – and got – planning permission to bulldoze it but there was such a national outcry that the funds were raised for the town to buy it back and hand it over to the National Trust. The old kitchen and the housekeeper's room now serve as a café/restaurant where you can get morning coffee, light lunches and afternoon tea.

Two other famous men were born in Eaglesfield, a mile from the town's centre: Fletcher Christian, the man who led the mutiny on the Bounty was born in 1764, and attended the same school as Wordsworth; then, in 1766 came John Dalton, a brilliant scientist and originator of the atomic theory.

Cockermouth Castle was built in the 13th century, but not much of it remains because of the efforts of Robert the Bruce and his marauding Scots. Most of the remaining ruins are from a later period, between 1360 to 1370.

Tourist Information Centre
Town Hall, Market Place,
Cockermouth, CA13 9NP
✆ 01900 822634

28

PLACES OF INTEREST

Jennings Brewery
Offers 1½ hour tours around its premises, pictured right, explaining the processes involved in brewing traditional beer.
- 0845 1297185
- www.jenningsbrewery.co.uk

The Museum of Printing
A fascinating range of printing presses brought together from all over Britain.
- 01900 824984

The Bitter End, *15 Kirkgate*
The first pub in Cumbria with its own working brewery – 'Cumbria's Smallest Brewery'.
- 01900 828993
- www.bitterend.co.uk.

Lakeland Sheep & Wool Centre
At the roundabout on the A66 is where you can meet Cumbria's most famous residents.

Western Lake District Visitor Centre
Tells you all about the area. It is also a hotel (see entry) .

Castlegate House
Contemporary art exhibitions.
- 01900 822149

The Toy & Model Museum
Mainly British toys from 1900 onwards.

WHERE TO EAT

Beatfords Country Restaurant
7 Lowther Went
- 01900 827099

Cheers Bistro
22, Main St
- 01900 822109

The Bitter End Brew Pub
15 Kirkgate
Excellent value, great beer and great food.
- 01900 828993

Junipers Restaurant & Cafe Bar
11 South St.
- 01900 822892

Quince & Medlar
13 Castlegate
Fine food – vegetarian.
- 01900 823579

Norham Coffee House & Restaurant
73 Main St
- 01900 824330

Oscar's Bistro
18-20 Market Place.
- 01900 823654

Nikki's Italian Restaurant & Bistro
7 Old Kings Arms Lane
- 01900 821223

Taste of India
4-5 Headford Court, Main Street
- 01900 827844

Lee's Chinese Takeaway and Fish & Chips
47 Main St
- 01900 827770

Rose Cottage

Lorton Road, Cockermouth,
Cumbria CA13 9DX
Run by: John and Susan Graham

A family run guest house in its own grounds. All rooms en-suite with colour TV, tea/coffee, central heating and all are now double glazed. Warm friendly atmosphere.

- ✆ 01900 822189
- 🖥 www.rosecottageguest.co.uk
- ✉ bookings@rosecottageguest.co.uk
- 🛏 4D, 3T, 2F, 1S
- 💷 £32.50–£45
- 🍽 Pk Lunch: from £6.50
- 🍽 Eve Meal: £22 for 3 courses
- 🚲 Dist from C2C 400m
- 🍺 Pubs nearby

Allerdale Court Hotel

Market Place, CA13 9NQ
Run by: John Carlin

Warm hostpitality, good food, comfort and dedicated attention to detail is what this family run establishment prides itself on. Cosy yet fashionable, the Allerdale welcomes cyclists, golfers and general holidaymakers with equal courtesy.

- ✆ 01900 823654
- 🖥 www.allerdalecourthotel.co.uk
- ✉ info@allerdalecourthotel.co.uk
- 🛏 5T, 4S, 12D/S
- 💷 £44-£72
- 🍽 Eve Meal: Pickwick: £17.95
  2-courses; £21.95 3-courses.
  Oscars Bistro: £5.95-£13.95
- 🍽 Pk Lunch: By arrangement

Riverside

12 Market St, Cumbria, CA13 9NJ
Run by: Rachel & Jean Habgood

Friendly, family run Georgian home with comfortable beds, excellent breakfasts, local amenities, tea-trays

and drying facilities plus bike lock-up.

- ✆ 01900 827504
- 🛏 2T, 1S
- 💷 £23-£25
- 🍽 Pk Lunch: £3.50
  (prior notice, please)
- 🚲 Dist from C2C: Right on C2C & Reivers routes

Try the Jennings Brewery for that special pit stop

Thornthwaite

DIRECTIONS

Leaving Cockermouth and on to Thornthwaite

Cross over Gote Street from the Papcastle road and continue past the James Walker factory, then right onto Bridge Street, crossing the river just after the doctor's surgery.

You then head left onto Main Street. Go past Station Street before turning right into Challoner Street, left into Cocker Lane and then almost immediately right to follow the river. Go under Lorton Street towards the Youth Hostel, turn right to swivel over the River Cocker and

COCKERMOUTH
route detail

Cockermouth tourist attractions include: Wordsworth House.

1 STATION STREET
2 LORTON STREET
3 VICTORIA ROAD
4 CHALLONER STREET
5 COCKER BRIDGE
6 STATION ROAD
7 WAKEFIELD ROAD
8 BRIDGE STREET

follow the path past the cemetery before the hairpin right turn onto Strawberry Home Road, where you take a left. It is now a straightforward run.

You may wish to stop near the shores of Bassenthwaite's northern tip, in which case go through the village of Wythop Mill and turn right by the phone box.

Turn left at the Pheasant Inn and go over the A66 onto the B5291, taking the scenic

Ouse Bridge to the Castle Hotel (listed in the Reivers section under Bassenthwaite).

It's a short hop up to the village and the Sun Inn, where they serve good food and ale.

Assuming you do not opt for this diversion, you will encounter a short, hilly section before the descent to Bassenthwaite Lake, from whence it is an easy ride into Keswick. At Thornthwaite you meet up with the Whitehaven route.

LEGEND OF BARF AND THE BISHOP

There is a Viking burial ground here at Powter Howe (review on next page) and just behind it is a hill called Barf.

You will see two large white rocks — one halfway up Barf, one at the bottom. The higher one is the Bishop, and the lower the Clerk. They commemorate the tale of a deadly 18th century drinking session at the Swan Inn (recently transformed into holiday apartments) during which the bibulous Bishop of Londonderry (doubtless on diocesan duty) bet his clerk that he could beat him to the top

of Barf. They downed their glasses and set off. The Right Reverend keeled over halfway up, the clerk pegged it at the bottom. The stones are said to commemorate this foolhardy wager. I do not know whether they were on their way up or down. Informed readers are welcome to write in.

Thornthwaite overlooks Bassenthwaite Lake, the only lake in the Lake District. This may seem strange, but all the other large expanses of H20 in the so-called Lake District are Waters, Meres or Tarns.

Powter Howe

Thornthwaite, Braithwaite,
nr Keswick, CA12 5SQ

Run by: Keren Lockwood

Reopened in July 2007. A 16th century farmhouse of great character with magnificent views over Bassenthwaite Lake towards Skiddaw. Set in two acres of mature garden, once visited never forgotten!

☎ 017687 78415

🛏 2D, 1T, 1S

💷 £25

🍴 Eve Meal: Pub 3km

🍴 Pk Lunch: By arrangement

Bassenthwaite Lake and its stunning view

Braithwaite

DIRECTIONS

Merging the routes from all the starting points

Nestling at the bottom of the Whinlatter Pass and Newlands Valley with the spectacular backdrop of Grisedale Pike and the Bassenthwaite Lake, the routes from Whitehaven / St Bees & Egremont and from Workington merge in time to take you to the picturesque village of Braithwaite.

Braithwaite is half way between Thornthwaite and Keswick. It's an excellent base for touring the Lake District, close to Loweswater, Crummock Water and Buttermere.

It's a straight and pleasant run through a quintessentially English village scene, over a Medieval humped-back bridge. This section of Braithwaite, leading out towards Little Braithwaite and Ullock, is somehow preserved in time. Only cars spoil the scene – otherwise you could be back in the 18th century.

CYCLE REPAIRS

Ian Hindmarch fixes bikes in his workshop next to the village stores , next to the hump-back bridge.

☏ 017687 78273.

Scotgate Holiday Park
Braithwaite, Keswick, CA12 5TF

A chalet, camping & caravan Park near Keswick. An outstanding holiday centre between Derwentwater and Bassenthwaite Lake on the threshold of the Lake District's most popular sites and with dramatic views towards Skiddaw and the northern fells. The perfect base, whether for a single night or taking a little more time.

☏ 017687 78343
🖥 scotgateholidaypark.co.uk
✉ info@scotgateholidaypark.co.uk
🚿 Shower, Laundry, Licensed Shop
☕ Coffee Shop, Braithwaite village 500m
🏠 Chalet rentals by arrangement

The Coledale Inn
Braithwaite, Nr. Keswick, Cumbria, CA12 5TN
Run by: Geoff & Charlie Mawdsley

A genuine country inn above in a peaceful hillside position well away from the traffic. It is ideal for both cycling and walking, with paths to the mountains from its gardens. Ideal spot for those not in a rush to explore the area.

☏ 017687 78272
🖥 www.coledale-inn.co.uk
✉ info@coledale-inn.co.uk
🛏 2S, 11D, 6T, 1F.
💷 £25-£36
🍽 Eve Meal: £7.50-£10.95
🍽 Pk Lunch: £4.50
🚲 Dist to C2C: On route

Keswick

DIRECTIONS

Braithwaite to Keswick

The route to Keswick via Portinscale is well signposted. You come into the town up the main street, following the traffic to the left and up to the lights at the Penrith Road. If not stopping in this delightful town, then go left down Station Street, turn right onto Brundholme Road, round in a loop and pick up the track heading east.

Sandwiched between Derwentwater, Blencathra and Skiddaw at the entrance to the mighty Borrowdale valley, this market town is blessed with one of Britain's most idyllic settings.

It is ideal for cycling, walking, boating or just sightseeing, and is a favourite venue with cycle back-up teams; it is the most popular and best-equipped stop-off point on the route.

Keswick ('Cese-Wic' - the Cheese Town, literally) became prosperous in the 17th century, during the reign of Elizabeth I, thanks to copper, lead, silver and iron mining.

There was so much work that engineers had to be imported from Germany. Despite a rocky start – at one stage, local xenophobia drove them to inhabit Derwent Island – they soon managed to integrate; evidence of this can be found in the phone book today, with its many Germanic surnames.

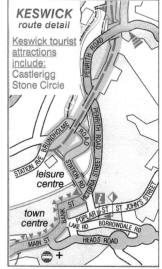

KESWICK *route detail*

Keswick tourist attractions include: Castlerigg Stone Circle

Drawing on the power of graphite

The town's Cumberland Pencil Company was established after the discovery of graphite in Borrowdale in the 16th century. However, the town was granted its charter some 300 years before that by Edward I in 1276.

Visitors started to flock in during the 18th century and Victorian times many of them were literary pilgrims, attracted by the association with such Romantic poets as Southey, Coleridge and Wordsworth. John Ruskin, the aesthete and champion of the Pre-Raphaelites, had close associations with the town.

The population of the place has grown little in the past century. In 1902 there were 4,500 people; now there are just 500 more, but many of them – as you will note if you choose to stop over – are B&B owners. The place also has many good pubs and solid restaurants.

CYCLE SHOPS

Keswick Bike Centre (Main store & Sales),
Otley Road, Keswick
☎ 01768 780856
🖥 www.KeswickBikes.co.uk

Keswick Bike Centre (Hire/Servicing)
Southey Hill, Keswick
☎ 01768 775202

PLACES OF INTEREST

Cumberland Pencil Museum
West of the town centre
☎ 017687 73626

Cars of the Stars
A pre-Carbon Footprint establishment. Famous cars including a James Bondmobile, the Batmobile and Chitty Chitty Bang Bang
☎ 017687 73757

Keswick Launch Company
Tours around Derwentwater
☎ 017687 72263.

George Fisher
Borrowdale Road
Big stock of outdoor gear, books and maps.
☎ 017687 72178

Cotswold Outdoor Ltd,
As above
☎ 017687 81939

The Moot Hall
Tourist Information Centre
☎ 017687 72645

Theatre by the Lake
Lakeside
Open all year round. Restaurant. Beautiful setting.
☎ 017687 74411

Alhambra Cinema
St.Johns Street
☎ 017687 72195

Keswick Museum & Art Gallery
Interesting and eclectic collection
☎ 017687 72263

Castlerigg Stone Circle
Thought to date from 3000BC Steep climb out of town on the alternative Penrith Road route. Worth the detour (pictured below)

PLACES TO EAT

Lemon & Lime
31 Lake Road
International cuisine with tapas, pizzas and other family favourites.
☏ 017687 73088

Salsa Mexican Bistro
1 New Street
Spicy and popular medium priced establishment owned by the Nellist brothers.
☏ 017687 75222

Swinside Inn
Newlands, Keswick
☏ 017687 78253

Red Fort Indian
5 St John Street
Lively and reliable spot very popular with the locals:
☏ 017687 74328

Luca's Ristorante
High Hill, Greta Bridge
Family run Italian with elaborate decoration and prices to match.
☏ 017687 74621

George Hotel
3 St John St
Medium priced fare:
☏ 017687 75751

Maysons Restaurant and Cafe
33, Lake Road,
Keswick, CA12 4AA
Simple and unpretentious eaterie. Good value for money.
☏ 017687 74104

Bank Tavern
47 Main Street
Solid, handsome pub with good, traditional English cooking. Medium price. Outside eating area for warm weather.
☏ 017687 72663.

CAFE & BIKES

The Lakeland Pedlar
Wholefood Cafe and Bicycle Centre, Bell Close, Keswick CA12 5JD
Great food, drink and bike accessories, all under the same roof.
☏ 017687 74492
💻 www.LakelandPedlar.co.uk

Powe House
Portinscale, Keswick, Cumbria CA12 5RW
Run by: Andrew & Helen Carey

Elegant Georgian house recently and lovingly restored. Bedrooms fully en-suite with LCD screens. All food is locally sourced and there is a solid and secure bike lock-up. Close to the well known Farmers Arms gastropub.
☏ 017687 73611
💻 www.powehouse.com
📧 andrewandhelen@powehouse.com
🛏 5D (3 of which can become twins) plus 1S
💷 From £32
🍽 Pk Lunch: from £4
ⓘ VisitBritain 4-stars Silver Award
🚲 Dist to C2C: On route

The Mount
Portinscale, Keswick, Cumbria CA12 5RD
Run by: Tony Mannion
Friendly, family run and comfortable B&B in quiet setting. En-suite rooms. Splendid lake/fell views. Excellent breakfasts with vegetarian option.
☏ 017687 73970
💻 www.mountferguson.co.uk
📧 mount.ferguson@virgin.net
🛏 1S,3D,1T.
💷 £32
🍽 Pk Lunch: £6
🚲 Distance to C2C: On route

Springs Farm
Springs Rd, CA12 4AN
Run by: Hazel Hutton

Comfortable accommodation in a large 19th century farmhouse at the foot of Walla Crag. This is a working dairy farm offering quality accommodation in an idyllic location but still only a 10 minute walk into town. It has been home to the Hutton family since 1924 and remains a family operated business. There is a pretty courtyard with ample parking. To the rear is a large orchard with apple, pear and plum trees, where free-range hens lay your breakfast eggs. There are also two cottages sleeping 6 and 2 available for rent.

- 017687 72144
- 07816 824253
- www.springsfarmcumbria.co.uk
- info@springsfarmcumbria.co.uk
- 2D, 1T
- £34-£36
- Nr pub: 1 mile to town centre
- VisitBritain 3 stars, 4 star cottages

The Queens Hotel
Main St, CA12 5JF

In the centre of town on the market square, and a hub of the action since being rebuilt in 1826. High standards of comfort and service in its 35 en-suite guest rooms. There is a secure lock-up for bikes and everything a tired cyclist needs. Recently and stylishly refurbished, there is an open fire in the bar.

- 017687 773333
- www.queenshotel.co.uk
- info@queenshotel.co.uk
- 5S, 12T/F, 18D
- from £40 (special deals available)
- Eve Meal: Bar meals—main courses £6-£8
- Pk Lunch: By arrangement

Pitcairn House
7 Blencathra St, CA12 4HW
Run by: Steve and Heather Hendy

Big and warm Victorian family run town house that has been a guest house since 1901. There is a secure area at the back for bikes and Steve and Heather welcome cyclists. Big fry in the morning if you wish.

- 017687 72453
- www.pitcairnhouse.co.uk
- enquiries@pitcairnhouse.co.uk
- 6 D/S, 1 T, 1 Tpl.
- £27.50-£32.50
- Pk Lunch: from £3.50 (please order in advance)
- Nr pub: 2 minutes walk

Cranford House
18 Eskin St, Keswick, CA12 4DG
Run by: Carol Hallgarth

Tasteful, doily-free, cycle friendly and comfortable stop-off. Just a couple of minutes from the town centre. Drying facilities and secure storage.

- 017687 71017
- www.cranfordhouse.co.uk
- carolcranfordhouse@tiscali.co.uk
- 2S, 3T/D,1D
- £25-£28
- Pk Lunch: £4

Honister House

1 Borrowdale Road, Keswick, Cumbria, CA12 5DD

Run by: John & Susie Stakes

"A warm welcome awaits you at our 18th century home in the centre of Keswick. Cyclists, walkers and families welcome. Drying room and storage. Award-winning breakfasts. Vegetarian options. Brochure available. One night occupation often available."

- ☎ 017687 73181
- 🖥 www.honisterhouse.co.uk
- ✉ honisterhouse@btconnect.com
- 🛏 1D, 1T, 1F
- 💷 £34–£37.
- 🍽 Pk Lunch: £4
- ⓘ AA 4-stars & AA Breakfast Award
- 🍺 Nr pub: 1 minute

Langdale Guest House

14 Leonard St, CA12 4EL

Run by: Lorraine Shipman

Secure area for bikes in this cycle friendly establishment, under new ownership since the end of 2006. Solid Victorian townhouse less than a minute's walk to the town centre. Veggie options for breakfast.

- ☎ 017687 73977
- 🖥 www.langdalekeswick.com
- ✉ s.g-s@tiscali.co.uk
- 🛏 2T, 3D, 1F
- 💷 £27-£32
- 🍽 Pk Lunch: £5

Beautiful Borrowdale is on your doorstep at Keswick

Twa Dogs Inn
Penrith Rd, CA12 4JU
Run by: Peter & Marjorie Harding & Family

"Traditional family run concern with an atmosphere as warm as the welcome. Open fires, dominoes, darts & pool in a proper pub. Lock-up for bikes and a range of real ales for their owners."

- 017687 72599
- www.twadogs.co.uk
- 1T, 1F (3S & 1D), 3D. (E-S).
- £30pp. Kids negotiable
- Eve Meal: From £6.95
- Pk Lunch: £5
- Dist to C2C: Just above railway line out of Keswick

Denton House
Penrith Rd, CA12 4JW
Run by: Cedric or Rebecca

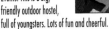

Budget accommodation run by Rebecca's bright new company, Vivid Events. This is a big, friendly outdoor hostel, full of youngsters. Lots of fun and cheerful.

- 01768 775351
- www.vividevents.co.uk
- sales@vividevents.co.uk
- 8 containing 58 bunk beds
- £13 during week. £14 weekends. Breakfast for groups of 10 or more: £3.
- Pk Lunch: £5 (groups only)
- Eve Meal: From £5 (groups only)
- Pub: 200m
- Dist to C2C: On route

Grassmoor Guest House
10 Blencathra Street
Keswick, CA12 4HP
Run by: Phil Heeley & Gillian Conroy

After a long day in the saddle settle down and relax with a complimentary cuppa in a comfortable en-suite room at Phil and Gillian's cycle-friendly Guest House. We offer a variety of substantial breakfasts to suit most appetites, a drying room, cycle wash, secure cycle storage and assistance with repairs.

- 017687 74008
- www.grassmoor-keswick.co.uk
- info@grassmoor-keswick.co.uk
- 4D/4T (en-suite), 2F, 2tpl
- £27 to £31
- Pk Lunch: from £4
- Distance to C2C: On route.
- Pubs and restaurants nearby

Beckside
5 Wordsworth Street, CA12 4HU
Run by: Tracey and Andrew Graham

Though it has been taken over by Tracy and Andrew, the fine cycling traditions of this establishment have been maintained right down to the (optional) killer breakfast. The parting fry-up has been described as all-embracing – but don't worry, you will soon be murdering these calories. wRooms en-suite, secure bike storage.

- 017687 73093
- www.beckside-keswick.co.uk
- info@beckside-keswick.co.uk
- 2D, 1T/F
- £26.50-£30
- Pk Lunch: On request—prior notice
- VisitBritain: 3-stars

39

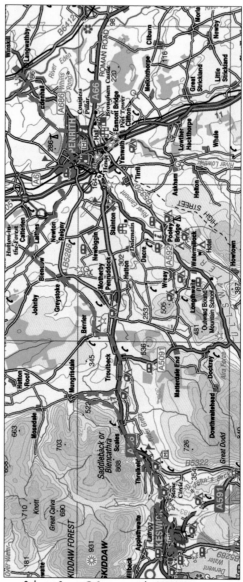

Ordnance Survey © Crown copyright: 100039985

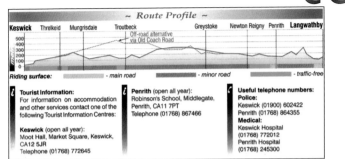

~ Route Profile ~

| Keswick | Threlkeld | Mungrisdale | Troutbeck | | Greystoke | Newton Reigny | Penrith | Langwathby |

Off-road alternative via Old Coach Road

Riding surface: ▬ - main road   ▬ - minor road   ▬ - traffic-free

Tourist Information:
For information on accommodation and other services contact one of the following Tourist Information Centres:

Keswick (open all year):
Moot Hall, Market Square, Keswick, CA12 5JR
Telephone (01768) 772645

Penrith (open all year):
Robinson's School, Middlegate, Penrith, CA11 7PT
Telephone (01768) 867466

Useful telephone numbers:
Police:
Keswick (01900) 602422
Penrith (01768) 864355
Medical:
Keswick Hospital
(01768) 772012
Penrith Hospital
(01768) 245300

DIRECTIONS AND ROUTE CHOICES

There are two ways out of Keswick. The most popular – and by far the easier – is the one that follows the old Keswick-Penrith railway line and the river Greta as far as Threlkeld. It is a beautiful and leafy stretch. You get to it down Station Road and Brundholme Road, bearing left at the swimming pool and heading in front of the old station.

The alternative takes you up into the hills above the town, but is only for the fit and even then watch the weather reports before taking to the upper slopes.

Both routes assume the same start, unless you want to go out of Keswick along the old Penrith road.

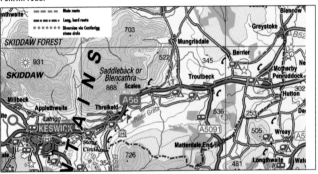

The hard one

If you're feeling energetic and (seriously) fit, try the Old Coach Road over the hills. It branches from the railway route, just before the track goes under the A66 viaduct, and goes up the steep slope to Castlerigg Stone Circle. Press on through St John's in the Vale, Matterdale End and down to Greystoke via Hutton John.

The Coach Road (what coach could possibly have tackled this?) is a seriously rough off-road alternative and very exposed. Check the weather before tackling it and don't do it if you're not certain of your capabilities.

There is accommodation where the route crosses the A5091 at Matterdale (see Troutbeck, and further along, just off the A66, Penruddock & Motherby) before the route rejoins the alternative at Greystoke.

The middle alternative

Start along the toughest route described above but after stopping to admire the Castlerigg circle, bear left down the hill and rejoin the more sedate option.

The main route

This takes you fairly effortlessly alongside the River Greta, all the way to Threlkeld.

41

Threlkeld & Scales

ABOUT THRELKELD

History from hunting to mining and back

Looking back to Blencathra

Blencathra, known locally as Saddle-back, overlooks this traditional and pretty village. There are also views towards Clough Head and the Helvellyn range.

Threlkeld is, I gather, Norse for 'the spring of the thrall' – thrall being a bonded servant. Zinc, lead and granite were mined during the last century until the last of the granite miners hung up their shovels and picks in the mid-80s.

At one time, there were more than a hundred men were employed in the mines and at the quarry there is a museum with an impressive mineral collection, mining artefacts and touching reminders of how things used to be.

A table top relief map of the Lake District and a pictorial history of Threlkeld are also on display. There was once a TB isolation hospital which is now a field centre for biologists and geographers.

Since the Dark Ages and the days of Sir Lancelot de Threlkeld, hunting has been an integral part of local life; this is the home of the Blencathra Hunt, the Lakeland pack that traditionally hunts on foot rather than on horseback and claims that its dogs are descended from those used by John Peel of song fame.

The Threlkeld sheepdog trials are a highlight of the year and feature foxhound and terrier shows, as well as hound training. All of these rural pursuits are, one presumes, finding life tougher these days.

The Hollies

Threlkeld, nr Keswick, CA12 4RX
Run by: John & Margaret Fleet
Fine stone-built house with spectacular views to front and rear. John & Margaret have been in the hotel business for 30 years so know how to look after you. Ample parking. Great breakfast. Bathrooms recently refurbished plus new deluxe room.

☎ 017687 79216 or 07887 611127
🖥 www.theholliesinlakeland.co.uk

✉ info@theholliesinlakeland.co.uk
🛏 4T/D
💷 £32.50-£35
🍴 Pk Lunch: £4

Horse & Farrier Inn
Threlkeld, nr Kewick, CA12 4SQ
Run by: Ian Court & Susan Whalley

The Horse & Farrier enjoys an idyllic location in the centre of the picturesque village of Threlkeld, just four miles east of Keswick. Built in 1688 at the foot of Blencathra, with stunning views. 'Cask Marque' Real Ales and extensive wine list are served in the bar, restaurant or beer garden. Excellent reputation for good food, using seasonal local produce always freshly prepared. Numerous recommendations include an AA two rosette accreditation. There is now a bigger bike storage area, increased drying facilities plus a cottage for rental next door.

- (017687 79688
- www.horseandfarrier.com
- enquiries@horseandfarrier.com
- 2S, 6D, 1T
- £35
- Eve Meal: £6.95-£15
- Pk Lunch: £5
- AA listed AA Hotel, Restaurant & Pub Guides

Horse & Farrier Guest House
Threlkeld, nr Keswick, Cumbria CA12 4SQ
Run by: Ian Court & Susan Whalley

Due to the enormous popularity of the Horse & Farrier Inn Ian and Susan have recently purchased additional accommodation to the Inn. The Horse & Farrier Guest House is opposite the pub's rear car park just a few seconds walk from the Inn and offers an additional four rooms. All the main services are offered in the Inn, such as breakfast, lunch and dinner. All the Horse & Farrier special offers apply to the guest house and all rooms offer tea & coffee making facilities, TV /DVD and hair dryers. There is a television lounge with DVD, reading books and a selection of board games. Additional facilities include: ironing board, drying room, bike lock up and newspapers. Large parties wishing to hire the facility for more than five days will get special rates.

- (017687 79688
- www.horseandfarrier.com
- enquiries@horseandfarrier.com
- 3T/D, 1D
- from £35
- Eve Meal: served at pub: £6.95-£15
- Pk Lunch: £5

Don't forget to look back and admire the view

NEXT STOP SCALES

After Threkeld there is a short section along a car-free country road, then a cycle path alongside the A66 until Scales, before you go along a delightful gated lane to Mungrisdale.

Don't forget to look up to admire Blencathra on your left and the Helvellyn range to the right.

Scales Farm Country Guest House

Scales, Threlkeld, Nr Keswick, CA12 4SY. Run by: Alan & Angela Jameison

Modernised 17th century Lakeland farmhouse at the foot of Blencathra overlooking the northern Lake District fells. Trad & vegetarian breakfasts. Immaculate throughout.

- ☎ 017687 79660
- 🖥 www.scalesfarm.com
- ✉ scales@scalesfarm.com
- 🛏 3D, 1F, 2T/D (E-S)
- 💷 £30-£37
- 🍽 Eve Meal: Pub next door
- 🍽 Pk Lunch: £4.50-£6
- ⓘ VisitBritain 4 stars Silver Award

Mungrisdale/Troutbeck

The delightful village of Mungrisdale comprises a traditional inn, a church and a cluster of houses all huddled around the bubbling river Glenderamackin.

A truly restful spot, as you reach it along the gated road you have spectacular views of the fells; Souther and Blencathra to the West and the Ullswater fells to the South – and to the east the daunting prospect of the Pennines.

The Sustrans route suggests you cross the river just short of the village, but that would be a shame. There is an alternative exit path over minor lanes, through Berrier and onto the Greystoke road, or follow the lane back down the other side of the Glendermackin to the A66, where the cycle path takes over.

At the top of the hill you can follow the route to the left or carry straight on for Greystoke. Either will do.

Troutbeck is about two miles further along the A66 once you have returned to it from Mungrisdale.

Be very careful crossing, though. Many a motorist attempts the land speed record on this stretch.v

---

Troutbeck Inn

Troutbeck, Penrith,
Cumbria, CA11 0SJ
Run by: Margaret & Neil Ward

Warm welcome in a large and relaxing Victorian hotel. All seven rooms are en-suite and there are three holiday cottages for rent for those wishing to explore the area. Real ale, family run bar and

restaurant and fine selection of malts to drive out the damp as you sit in front of the log fire.

✆ 017684 83635
🖥 www.thetroutbeckinn.co.uk
✉ troutbeckinn1@btconnect.com
🛏 1S, 4D, 1T, 1F
💷 £32.50-£50
🍽 Eve Meal: £6.50-£10.95
🍽 Pk Lunch: From £5

Blencathra and Skiddaw

Motherby & Penruddock

Herdwick Inn

Penruddock, CA11 OQU.
Run by: Linda & Mark Wilmot
Traditional 18th century country inn with log fire offering good home cooked food from locally ingredients. Great duck and lamb, or local pies. Sunday carvery is very popular. A warm welcome and fine real ales. Rooms recently refurbished and have en-suite facilities. On B5288 to Greystoke, the alternative increasingly popular route via Motherby.
☎ 01768 483007

🖥 www.herdwickinn.com
✉ info@herdwickinn.com
🛏 1T, 3D, 1S
💷 £37.50-£47.50
🍽 Eve Meal: £6.95-£13
🍽 Pk Lunch: from £4 (notice preferred)
ⓘ VisitBritain 4 stars

Motherby House

Motherby,nr Penrith,
Cumbria CA11 ORJ
Run by: Jacquie Freeborn
Warm, friendly former 18th century farmhouse. Excellent food for outdoor appetites and muddy clothes welcome.

☎ 017684 83368
🖥 motherbyhouse.co.uk
✉ jacquie@
   motherbyhouse.co.uk

🛏 2F
💷 £24.50
🍽 Eve Meal: £16 3 courses
🍽 Pk Lunch: £6.50
🍸 Nr pub: 1.5km

Blencow Hall, a landmark near Greystoke

Greystoke

ABOUT THE VILLAGE

Paying homage to the original Tarzan

This traditional English village, 8km west of Penrith, was built around a green with a pretty pub and a church the size of a cathedral.

Discretely hidden at the top of a long drive and behind a curtain of trees in a 3,000 acre wooded park is Greystoke Castle, seat of the Howard family since the 1500s when they were emerging as movers and shakers behind the monarchies of the late Tudors and early Stuarts.

Tarzan is modelled on one former Baron Greystoke, and there are certainly enough trees for any Lord of the Apes to practice on. It is a family home and business rather than a theme park, so not much is made of the Tarzan link, but I thought Tarzan fans might be interested.

The village is probably Roman in origin, lying alongside the road they built from Penrith to Troutbeck. The name means 'place by the River Creik', a small stream nearby. The village was known as Creistock in early Medieval times.

Though most of the village dates from the 17th century, the foundation of the Perpendicular-style church was laid in the mid-1200s, though building did not start until 1382 and went on into the next century. The bells that still ring out in Greystoke date from the Middle Ages. Inside is some fine Medieval and Victorian stained glass (see picture).

The Spillers Stone in the village was thought to be a plague stone, where plague victims left coins in a pool of vinegar on its concave surface. The vinegar was supposed to protect the healthy, who left food there for sufferers.

According to the Cumbria Directory, Greystoke Castle was an integral part of village life, the first version being constructed in 1129 as protection against Scottish Border raiders, early versions of the Reivers, that came to dominate the area before the cycle route picked up the nomenclature.

Cromwell destroyed much of Greystoke and a devastating fire in 1868 ensured that only the medieval pele (fortified) tower and a few Georgian interiors survived and the present building, though it mimics the Elizabethan style, actually dates from the 19th century.

The nearby countryside boasts a number of fine old fortified houses complete with pele towers, notably Blencow Hall, built in 1590, Greenthwaite Hall, and Johnby Hall. All are reminders of the bloody times in the Borders.

The Boot and Shoe Pub in the village acquired its name because of the strange sartorial habit of a former Duke of Norfolk of wearing a shoe on one foot and a boot on the other, to ease the pain of crippling gout. Whether or not, thus clad, he shuffled down the long drive and across the green to the pub is not recorded.

He would have done better settling for tea and scones at Annie Swarbrick's Greystoke Cycle Cafe (see entry), a welcome addition to the village.

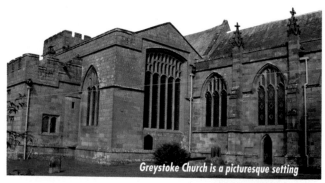
Greystoke Church is a picturesque setting

Stafford House

Greystoke Castle, Greystoke
Run by: Hazel Knight

Large Victorian folly that looks like a walled Gothic castle within the grounds of Tarzan's castle (Greystoke) and shares the same magnificent drive. The listed house sits in ¾ of an acre of its own grounds with castle battlements on three sides and arched windows. Aside from looking Medieval, it is very comfortable.

- 017684 83558
- 07759 133281
- hazel.knight@btconnect.com

- 2D, 1T.
- £30-£32.50
- Pk Lunch: from £4
- Nr pub: half an arrow flight
- Grade II listed

The Bunkhouse

Stafford House, Greystoke Castle, Greystoke, Cumbria
Run by: Hazel Knight

This new bunkhouse, hopefully opening in June 2008, will sleep up to 16 in two dormitories, Saddleback Lodge and Pennine Lodge. The head gardener for Greystoke Castle used to reside in the main house at this property and used the lodge to store all the home-grown fruit and supplies for the Howard family through the long winters. It is now fully kitted out with a fitted kitchen-diner, with every convenience including linen and towels, wet rooms, drying rooms, lock-

ers are available and one of the toilets is converted for the disabled. Tea, coffee, fruit juice, various cereals and milk are provided. The rest can be found at the local shop, which is only 5 minutes walk and offers a good choice of fare, the Boot & Shoe pub or the Cycle Cafe.

- Contact details same as Stafford House
- Saddleback dorm: sleeps 4-6, Blencathra dorm: sleeps 8-10
- £15
- Nr pub: 400 yards
- Location: Grounds of Greystoke Castle, next to Stafford House

Boot & Shoe

Greystoke, Penrith,
Cumbria CA11 0TP

Run by: Jan & Ben Mandale

Since Jan, Ben and Susie took over in July 2007 the Boot & Shoe has enjoyed a new lease of life. There's a real buzz about the place; cyclists, jockeys and locals jostle for place while Jan hands out steaming plates of excellent food ranging from chicken balti to local dishes like Lamb Henry. A real community hub. Log fire in the bar, stove in the lounge plus selection of well kept real ales.

- ☎ 017684 83343
- 🖥 www.boot-and-shoe.com
- ✉ mandale@lineone.net
- 🛏 4T+1D/T (en-suite)
- 💷 £30-£37.50
- 🍴 Eve Meal: £5.95-£12.95 (main courses)

Keswick – Langwathby

Greystoke Cycle Cafe

CA11 0UT

Run by: Annie Swarbrick

This is a splendid little stop off for a nice summer's day, or take shelter in the barn if it's not so nice. Annie's garden is a lovely spot and the home baked cakes, scones, paninis, bacon butties and home made soups are a treat. Tea, coffee, cold drinks and all the essentials you could imagine at this delightful pitstop just a stone's throw from the village green. Annie organises all sorts of activities from this old farmhouse—just take a look at 'Quirky Workshops' on the

website. The Cyclists' Barn' is open 10–6pm with hot drinks /cakes solely for those on bicycles. Great views across parkland to Greystoke Castle. Car/van parking for C2C support drivers only.

- ☎ 017684 83984
- 🖥 www.greystokecyclecafe.co.uk
- ✉ annie@greystokecyclecafe.co.uk

Brathen

The Thorpe, Greystoke, nr
Penrith, Cumbria CA11 0TJ

Run by: Christine Mole

Comfortable barn conversion on the outskirts of the village with a warm wel-

come and hearty breakfasts using local produce.

- ☎ 017684 83595

- 🖥 www.brathen.co.uk
- ✉ stay@brathen.co.uk
- 🛏 2D, 2T, 2F
- 💷 £25
- 🍴 Pk Lunch: £4
- 🚲 On C2C route
- 🍺 Nr pub: 300 yds

49

Penrith
DIRECTIONS

Leaving Greystoke, then on to Newton Reigny and Penrith

The route out of Greystoke goes past Blencow Hall, the aforementioned fortified farmhouse. It is an unusually handsome building just before you get to the village of Little Blencow. Just up the road follow signs to the right and you will enter Penrith via Newton Reigny and Newton Rigg.

On leaving Newton Rigg campus go underneath the M6 and turn right at the T-junction, going into town along Robinson Street, across Scotland Rd and into Drover's Lane.

The route is well sign-posted.

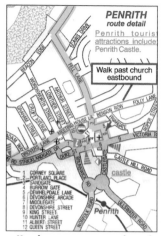

PENRITH
route detail

Penrith tourist attractions include: Penrith Castle.

Walk past church eastbound

1 CORNEY SQUARE
2 PORTLAND PLACE
3 SANDGATE
4 BURROW GATE
5 DEWHELPDALE LANE
6 DEVONSHIRE ARCADE
7 MIDDLEGATE
8 DEVONSHIRE STREET
9 KING STREET
10 HUNTER LANE
11 ALBERT STREET
12 QUEEN STREET

You know you are on the right tracks when you find yourself exiting Penrith up Fell Lane – a steep climb to a T-junction at the top.

ABOUT THE TOWN

Home to a legendary giant, a would-be king and a poet

A handsome red sandstone market town, Penrith was the capital of the Kingdom of Cumbria in the 9th and 10th centuries, a time when the area was allied to Scotland as a semi-independent part of the Kingdom of Strathclyde. Since it was on the main north-south road it also witnessed more than its fair share of bloody action during border conflicts; the Scots put the town to torch three times during the 14th century alone.

Its early growth was restricted because the town had no water supply but in 1385 Bishop Strickland diverted Thacka Beck from the river Peterill, an eco-sensitive agreement that allowed the townspeople to draw only as much water daily from the Peterill as would flow through the eye of a millstone, still on view outside the Tourist Information Centre.

By the 18th century it was an important cattle market. The oldest streets in the town, Burrowgate and Sandgate, are narrow, unspoilt and 800 years old. Two traditional shops have also survived, as if preserved in aspic: Graham's, Penrith's answer to Fortnum & Mason; and Arnisons, the drapers, established in 1740 in the building that was once the home of Wordsworth's grandparents. The poet and his sister, Dorothy attended the Dame Anne Birkett School, now the Tudor Coffee Room, overlooking St Andrew's Churchyard and final resting place of Owen Caesarius, a legendary giant and King of All Cumbria.

They are far from the only famous figures from history associated with the town. As "Guardian of the West March towards Scotland" the Duke of Gloucester plotted his way towards being crowned Richard III of England, from behind the sandstone ramparts of the magnificent Penrith Castle.

It was not all sculduggery though: he also stayed at one of the pubs in town and is even said to have had a private underground passage to it so that he could go back and forth unseen. The link is commemorated in the pub's name, the Gloucester Arms, and some of the original stonework is still there – which is scarcely true of the castle which was a ruin by the mid 16th century, donating much of its stonework to the town's buildings.

The Two Lions pub is equally historic while the George Hotel provided lodgings for Bonnie Prince Charlie in 1745 during his ill-fated foray south in search of the crown.

Others linked to Penrith include Mary Queen of Scots, Oliver Cromwell and the writer, Anthony Trollope. The first must have spent most of her life on horseback to get to all the places she is alleged to have visited, though in the case of Penrith the connection is justified. Cromwell, occupied the town in 1654 and though the pen is mightier than the sword Trollope is not thought to have caused as much bloodshed. More recently, the area was immortalised in Bruce Robinson's classic film comedy of 1987, 'Withnail and I', in which the area is again traumatised – this time by a pair of drunken wannabe actors.

Above Penrith is Beacon Hill, past which you will shortly be cycling. Beacons have been lit there through the ages to warn of threat of invasion. Its views are stunning.

THINGS TO SEE

Penrith Museum and Tourist Information Centre
Housed in the former Robinson's School, an Elizabethan building altered in 1670 and a school until the early 1970s. The museum covers the history, geology and archaeology of the Penrith area. Free entry.

✆ 01786 867466

St Andrew's Church
The Giant's Grave in the Churchyard is that of Owen Caesarius, the legendary slayer of monsters from Inglewood Forest. The tower is 12th century, the rest dates from 1720, being rebuild after a fire with the stained-glass windows added in 1870.

Bluebell Bookshop,
Angel Square
✆ 01768 866660.

The town's architecture
Take a walk around. Well worth a stopover.

Penrith Castle
Started in 1399, once home to Richard III but abandoned after his death. Free entry

PLACES TO EAT

Fifteen
15 Victoria Road
A welcome addition to the Penrith food scene. Laid back atmosphere. Food is fresh and simple yet inventive. Healthy options and some fine cake. Cycle enthusiasts.

✆ 01768 867453

Bewicks Coffee Shop & Bistro
Princes Court
Accomplished and simple; lovely setting, reasonable prices.

✆ 01768 864764

Taste of Bengal
Stricklandgate
Solid and unpretentious dishes from a place without pretentions.

✆ 01768 891700

Peaberrys Restaurant & Cafe
Angel Square
Smart in-and-out eaterie, reasonable prices.

✆ 01768 890170

George Hotel
Devonshire Street
Does everything from lounge snacks to formal restaurant. It's both reliable and reasonable.

✆ 01768 862696

Platinum Chinese Restaurant
The buffet is more than adequate. There have been some rave reports from other diners.

✆ 01768 210210

Blue Elephant Café
Angel Square
A vegetarian organic retreat to be found upstairs from the Bluebell Bookshop. New cafe owner.

✆ 01768 866660.

Scotts Fish Restaurant
Sandgate
53-seat no-nonsense chippie next to the bus station

✆ 01768 890838.

Fellfoot
10 Fell Lane, CA11 8AA
Run by: Alasdair & Jackie Rutherford

Fellfoot Independent is a recently opened hostel facility in the centre of town 85 km from the start of the C2C. Fellfoot offers welcoming and budget facilities for those determined souls in transit. There are four twin rooms, self catering facilities, private garden and secure Bike Storage. Also offers self-catering or bed and buffet breakfast accommodation. Prices from £18.50 Availability all year round. We look forward to seeing you.

- ☎ 01768 840327
- 🖥 www.fellfoot.com
- ✉ ajruther4rd@homecall.co.uvk
- 🛏 4T
- 💷 £20 (bed alone); £23.50 (B&B)
- 🍴 Nr pub: 2 minutes

Brandelhow Guest House
1 Portland Place, Penrith, Cumbria CA11 7QN
Run by: Lanie and Mel Hancox
Victorian town house, close to the town centre, ideally situated for the C2C cycle route and walking holidays in the Lakes.

- ☎ 01768 864470
- 🖥 www.brandelhowguesthouse.co.uk
- ✉ enquiries@brandelhowguesthouse.co.uk
- 🛏 1S, 2D/T, 1T, 2F (one sleeps six).
- 💷 £30
- 🍴 Pk Lunch: £6
- 🚲 Dist to C2C: On route
- 🍴 Pub nearby
- ⓘ 4 star AA VisitBritain

Roundthorn Country House
Beacon Edge, Penrith, CA11 8JS
Run by: Graham Carruthers
A beautiful Georgian mansion with spectacular views of the Eden Valley & Lakeland Fells. All rooms are en-suite with TV and tea/coffee making facilties. The hotel has a licensed bar and is great value for money for a hotel of this class.

- ☎ 01768 863 952
- 📠 01768 864 100
- 🖥 www.roundthorn.co.uk
- ✉ info@roundthorn.co.uk
- 🛏 7D, 2T, 2F (E-S).
- 💷 £47.50–£67 (licensed)
- 🍴 Pk Lunch: £6.50
- 🍴 Eve Meal: £8.50–£10.50
- 🚲 Dist to C2C: On route.
- 🍴 Nr Pub: bar in hotel
- ⓘ VisitBritain 5 star guest accommodation

Glendale

4 Portland Place, Penrith, Cumbria CA11 7QN
Run by: Moira & Allan Sutcliffe

Spacious rooms with friendly, comfortable atmosphere. Ideal stopover where, after a good night's rest, the famous Glendale hearty breakfast will set you up for the climb to Alston and beyond! Pets welcome.

- ☏ 01768 862579
- 🖥 www.glendaleguesthouse.com
- ✉ glendaleguesthouse@yahoo.co.uk
- 🛏 1S, 2D, 4T/ 4F
- 💷 £30-£35.
- 🍽 Pk Lunch: from £4.00
- 🚲 Distance t6 C2C: On route
- 🍺 Pub nearby
- ⓘ VisitBritain 4 stars AA 4 stars

Eden Gate

5 Victoria Road, Penrith, CA11 8HR
Run by: Lorraine Roberts

'S.Rhodes & party from Teesside left the following note: "Excellent stop for C2Cers – unable to fault." You too can enjoy their comfortable rooms, delicious breakfast, secure cycle parking.

Within two to three minutes walk of shops and restaurants. Groups of up to 10 catered for.'

- ☏ 01768 866538
- 🖥 edengateguesthouse.co.uk
- ✉ enquire@edengateguesthouse.co.uk
- 🛏 1D, 1T, 2F
- 💷 £28—£40
- 🍺 Nr pub 100m
- ⓘ Drying and secure lock-up

Acorn Guest House

Scotland Rd, Penrith, CA11 9HL
Run by: Joyce & Anita

Cycle friendly, immaculate family run guest house five minutes walk from the

town centre. Sizeable rooms are airy and clean with colour TV. Full English breakfast using good local pigs.

- ☏ 01768 868696
- 🖥 www.acorn-guesthouse.co.uk
- ✉ acornguesthouse@fsmail.net
- 🛏 4D,4T,1F
- 💷 £29.50-£35
- 🍽 Eve Meal: Groups only catered for
- 🍽 Pk Lunch: £4.50
- 🚲 Dist to C2C: On route
- 🍺 Nr pub: 50m
- ⓘ AA 4 stars
- ⓘ Secure lock-up

Caledonia Guest House

8 Victoria Road, Penrith, CA11 8HR
Run by: Ian & Sue Rhind

Family run Victorian town house with spacious rooms. Good hearty breakfast in a warm and friendly atmosphere. TV, tea and coffee making facilities in all rooms.

- ☏ 01768 864 482 (also fax)
- 🖥 www.caledonia guesthouse.co.uk
- ✉ ian.rhind1@virgin.net
- 🛏 2D, 3T, 1F
- 💷 £29—£35
- 🍽 Pk Lunch: £5.00
- 🍺 Nr pub: 200m

Albany House

5 Portland Place, Penrith,
Cumbria CA11 7QN
Run by: Susan Bell

Lovely mid-Victorian town house close to town centre. Hospitality tray, drying facilities, secure bike storage. Hearty breakfast and the warmest of welcomes.

- ☎ 01768 863072
- 🖥 www.albany-house.org.uk
- ✉ info@albany-house.org.uk
- 🛏 2D, 3F.
- 💷 £27.50-£40
- 🍽 Pk Lunch: From £2.30
- 🚲 Dist to C2C: On route
- 🍺 Pub nearby
- ℹ 3 star AA, Highly Commended

Norcroft Guest House

Graham Street Penrith, Cumbria CA11 9LQ
Run by: Paul Lamb

Family run, licensed guest house in a large Victorian house, accommodating up to 22 guests. Secure covered storage for bikes.

- ☎ 01768 862365
- 🖥 www.norcroft-guesthouse.co.uk
- ✉ info@norcroft-guesthouse.co.uk
- 🛏 1S, 7T, 3F, 1Tpl
- 💷 from £32.50
- 🍽 Pk Lunch: from £4
- 🚲 Distance to C2C: On route
- 🍺 Nr pub 200m
- ℹ VisitBritain 4-stars. Warm Welcome Award and Fully licensed
- ℹ Drying facilities   Yes
- ℹ Secure lock up   Yes

Abbey House

7 Victoria Road, Penrith, Cumbria, CA11 8HR
Run by: Mark and Anne Holliday

Just 5 minutes walk from the town and close to the route. Four en-suite bedrooms with TVs and tea/coffee trays which can accommodate groups of up to 12. English breakfast. Secure lock up for cycles.

- ☎ 01768 863414
- 🖥 www.abbeyhousebandb.co.uk
- ✉ anneabbeyhouse@aol.com
- 🛏 4 D/T two of which can be triples
- 💷 £28-£35
- 🍽 Eve Meal: Pubs and restaurants nearby
- 🍽 Pk Lunch: from £4
- 🍺 Nr pub: 50m
- 🚲 Dist to C2C: 250m.
- ℹ Secure cycle storage

Blue Swallow Guest House

11 Victoria Road, Penrith, Cumbria, CA11 8HR
Run by: Peter and Cynthia Barry

Clean, comfortable rooms, en suite or private facilities, colour TV, Tea/Coffee trays. Excellent English breakfast using local produce. Secure lock up for cycles. Easy access to eating and drinking establishments. Well recommended with lots of repeat business.

- ☎ 01768 866335
- 🖥 www.blueswallow.co.uk
- ✉ blueswallow@tiscali.co.uk
- 🛏 3D, 5T, 2S, 3F (6 en-suite, one with private facilities)
- 💷 £29-£40
- 🍽 E meal: surrounded by pubs and restaurants
- 🍽 Pk Lunch: £5
- 🚲 Dist to C2C: 300m
- 🍺 Nr pub: 50m
- ℹ Open all year

Langwathby

DIRECTIONS

Last chance to take it easy before the serious stuff starts

You leave Penrith along Fell Lane before turning right onto Beacon Edge. There are fabulous views from here followed by a long descent to the B6412. Enjoy it while you can; the really serious bit is about to start.

Around Langwathby are the villages of Great Salkeld, Edenhall and Little Salkeld. If you are overnighting at Great Salkeld (the food at the Highland Drove is exceptional and the place is in the Michelin good pub food guide) then take a left along the B6412 for 3km. Great Salkeld is a pretty little village and the pub does B&B.

If you turn right onto the B6412 you are soon in the village of Edenhall, where the Eden Hall Country House offers splendid accommodation and fine cooking. Both villages are close to Langwathby, with its lovely village green and Shepherd pub. The nearest B&B to Langwathby itself is just out of the village, at Little Salkeld. The Atkinsons run an equine centre with accommodation. Clive and Sam are still doing some accommodation at Langstanes in the village, but said they were winding down.

There's a railway station that services the popular Carlisle to Settle line. This area is popular for overnight stops because the villages are well-placed for attacking Hartside and the other hills that make the next section the hardest. Melmerby, on the A686 about 5km from Langwathby is also popular. There's a pub there, a famous bakery, but limited B&B.

Langwathby was a Viking settlement; Edenhall once boasted a fine stately home and Little Salkeld, had its watermill. They are all close to the Long Meg and Little Meg stone circles.

Long Meg, pictured below, comprises a megalith at the head of 60 stones. The whole monument is some 360ft (115m) in diameter.

The Highland Drove Inn & Kyloes Restaurant

Great Salkeld, Langwathby, Penrith, CA11 9NA
Run by: Donald Newton

A real country pub with open fires, real ale, quality wines and beer garden. Excellent bar food with separate 'Kyloes' restaurant serving eclectic and award winning cuisine. Winner of Cumbria Dining Pub of the Year plus CAMRA's Real Ale Pub of the Year. Also in the Michelin 'inns with restaurants' guide. Top spot with well chosen wine list with a new pub, the Cross Keys, opening on the edge of Penrith.

- 01768 898349
- www.highland-drove.co.uk

- highlanddroveinn@btinternet.com
- 3D, 2T
- £35-£65
- Eve Meal: Bar: 2-courses £12. Restaurant 2-courses £20
- Pk Lunch: £7.50
- Dist to C2C 3km—but worth every inch.

Eden Hall Country Hotel & Restaurant

Edenhall, Langwathby, CA11 8SX
Run by: Paula & Wayne Williams

Star country house hotel in beautiful surroundings. Sky TV, telephone, tea/coffee in all rooms. Great chef. Secure cycle storage and drying facilities. Telephone for brochure. The new owners have introduced a very affordable and high end table d'hote (£19.50 for three courses).

- 01768 881454
- www.edenhallhotel.co.uk
- info@edenhallhotel.co.uk
- 5S, 9D, 7T (E-S).
- from £40, dinner B&B from £59.50
- Eve Meal: £7.95-£19.50 (table d'hote)
- Pk Lunch: £4.95
- VisitBritain: 2 star hotel

Bank House Farm

Little Salkeld, Langwathby, Penrith CA10 1NN
Run by: Raymond & Nancy Atkinson

B&B, self-catering or camping in converted barns and farm cottages for individuals, families or larger groups. Static 39-foot caravan accommodation now available so can take large groups. A warm friendly family welcome awaits whatever the chosen style of accommodation. Also has secure cycle storage.

- 01768 881257
- 07878 536892
- bankhouseequ@aol.com
- Lots of possibilities for individuals and groups
- £30
- Nr pub: 2km

Keswick – Langwathby

57

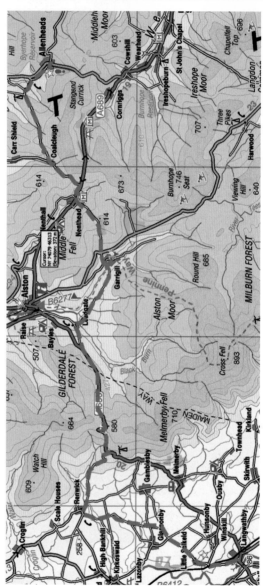

Ordnance Survey © Crown copyright: 100039985

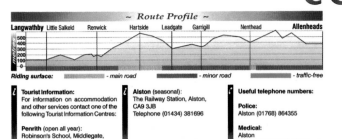

~ Route Profile ~

Langwathby Little Salkeld Renwick Hartside Leadgate Garrigill Nenthead **Allenheads**

500
400
300
200
100
0

Riding surface: ▬▬▬ - main road   ▬▬▬ - minor road   ▬▬▬ - traffic-free

Tourist Information:	Alston (seasonal):	Useful telephone numbers:
For information on accommodation and other services contact one of the following Tourist Information Centres:	The Railway Station, Alston, CA9 3JB Telephone (01434) 381696	Police: Alston (01768) 864355
Penrith (open all year): Robinson's School, Middlegate, Penrith, CA11 7PT Telephone (01768) 867466		Medical: Alston (Cottage Hospital Surgery) (01434) 381214

Kirkoswald

DIRECTIONS

To divert to Eden; or not to divert to Eden. That is the question

Although not directly on the C2C route, Kirkoswald sees a fair amount of cycle traffic meandering slightly from the set path to enjoy the Eden Valley.

When you exit Langwathby you will be presented with choices about what route to take.

🚲 The first sees you head back to milemarker 57 that you passed on the way into the village, turning onto the quiet road through Great Salkeld, Lazonby and over the River Eden before reaching Kirkoswald.

All the others st art by heading north towards Little Salkeld and Glassonby.

🚲 If you are taking the detour to Kirkoswald, leave the main C2C route at milemarker 61.5, head through Glassonby and down the hill into Kirkoswald. Make your way back to the route proper via Viol Moor running parallel to the Raven Beck and onto Four Lane End at milemarker 64.2.

🚲 If you decide to forego the joys of Kirkoswald, just plough straight up the main route and you are soon at Four Lane End.

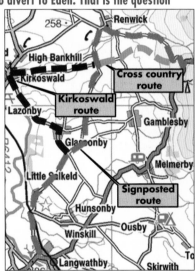

🚲 At Four Lane End you can turn right onto the cross-country route over Hartside, but if you do, be warned, you will be pushing or carrying your bike for a lot of the stretch.

🚲 The alternative takes you to Renwick, a winding and steep ascent (I suspect I am not the only cyclist to have hopped out of the saddle for a rest a couple of times).

Langwathby to Allenheads

59

ABOUT THE VILLAGE

Tribute to a warrior, king and saint

The village derives its name from St Oswald who was king of Northumberland from 634 to 642, re-establishing Christianity in the region, founding of the monastery at Lindisfarne and to whom the local church is dedicated. The church and bell tower are two separate buildings with the bell tower standing atop a conical hill above the church.

Just outside the village is Kirkoswald Castle, said once to have been "one of the fairest fabrics that eyes looked upon, having a great hall, one hundred yards long, ornamented with pictures of all the kings of England". Though not much remains today it is still worth the short walk to visit it.

Raven Beck, which runs through the village and near much of the path back to the main route, once powered three corn mills, a paper mill, and a mill for carding and spinning wool. It is now the centrepiece of a picturesque stroll above the village.

The Crown Inn

Kirkoswald, Penrith, Cumbria CA10 1DQ
Run by: Stella & Jeff Harling

A warm welcoming country pub serving food all day. Specialises in fresh egg pastas with carbohydrates, perfect for those on the go! Laundry service, bicycle maintenance and secure storage. Both Jeff and Stella are qualified chefs and their son James will be available for bicycle maintenance during the summer.

- (01768 870028
- jeffjharling@aol.com
- 2D, 2T
- £35-£45

- Pk Lunch: from £5
- Eve Meal: from £10.95
- Secure storage
- Drying facilities

Edendale Bed and Breakfast

Edendale, Kirkoswald, nr Penrith, Cumbria, CA10 1EN.
Run by: Mrs Jane Cottam

The comfortable en-suite rooms have stunning views, central heating, television and tea/coffee making facilities. The local shop and two pubs/restaurants are less than 5 minutes walk away. Edendale has a large lounge/dining room with an open fire.

- (01768 870127
- www.edendalebedandbreakfast.co.uk
- info@edendalebedandbreakfast.co.uk
- 1T, 1D, 1S (all en-suite)
- £28
- Pk Lunch: from £5
- Eve Meal: Two pubs serve food
- Nr pub: two within 200 yards
- Dist to C2C: 2miles

The Fetherston Arms
The Square, Kirkoswald, Cumbria, CA10 1DF
Run by: Jennifer & Glen Mossop

Over the years the Fetherston has offered a warm welcome, fine food and real ales to passing cyclists. It is a busy local pub and established guesthouse serving an extensive daily menu of traditional food and a choice of three local real ales. All rooms have been recently refurbished to a high standard with en-suite, tea/coffee making facilities and Freeview TV. There are washing/drying facilities as well.

- 01768 898284
- www.thefetherstonarms.co.uk
- info@thefetherstonarms.co.uk
- 1 deluxe D, 3D, 1S (all en-suite)

- £30-£35
- Pk Lunch: Yes
- Eve Meal: From £7. Extensive menu
- Open: all year
- Secure cycle storage

OUSBY AND MELMERBY

Bradley Foot
Ousby, nr Penrith, Cumbria, CA10 1QA
Run by: Meryl Durdy

Former 18th century farmhouse on outskirts of quiet fellside village, relaxing and peaceful with excellent views. Ideally situated for touring Lakes, Pennines and Northern Dales. Locked building for bikes. Drying facilities available. Full english breakfast with locally produced ingredients.

- 01768 881778 (also fax)
- bradleyfoot@hotmail.co.uk
- 2D, 1S (1 en-suite)
- £26
- Nr pub: 100m
- Dist to C2C: 3 miles from Hartside climb
- Secure cycle storage
- Open February-November

Meadow Bank
Melmerby, Cumbria, CA10 1HF
Run by: Mrs Margaret Morton

Meadow Bank is the last B&B you will come to on the west side of Hartside Pass. After a comfortable sleep followed by a hearty Cumbrian Breakfast, you will be ready to tackle the the rigours of Hartside Summit (2000ft).

- 01768 881652
- 1D, 1F (1 en-suite)
- £25
- Nr pub: 75m, serves good food
- Melmerby bakery nearby
- Secure storage
- Dist to C2C: 2 miles to the start of the Hartside climb

Alston

DIRECTIONS

Up Hartside, and back down again

Whichever way you go, it is a hard climb from Little Salkeld but at the top awaits Hartside Café, a (motor)bikers haven. At 580 metres (1900 feet), it is the highest tea shop in England and on a fine day (they do happen) you can see across the Solway Firth to Scotland. The views of the Eden Valley are terrific: not for nothing was the drive along the A686 voted one of the ten best in the world by the AA.

Your climb is rewarded by one of the best sections of downhill in the North West. Near the bottom of Benty Hill there is a road on the right heading towards Leadgate and Garrigill. You have a choice – take it, or continue the delirious descent along the A686 until you get to the handsome town of Alston, perched on the edge of the Pennines.

ABOUT THE VILLAGE

Picture perfect legacy of the lead mines

Alston sits at 280m (919feet) above sea level and is supposedly the highest market town in England. Picture-postcard-pretty and a firm favourite with outdoor types, it lies in an Area of Outstanding Natural Beauty (AONB), a solid bastion of civilisation on the edge of one of Britain's greatest areas of wilderness.

Once a centre for Cumberland wrestling, cattle fairs and races, Alston is unspoilt by developers and has cobbled streets, 17th century shops and pubs that hark back to a former age. Naturally it is a magnet for film makers; Oliver Twist was shot here for television – there is even an Oliver Twist trail – and Dickens himself visited in the 1830s to research Nicholas Nickleby.

The town, formed around the confluence of the South Tyne and Nent rivers, owes much to lead mining, started by the Romans before the Quakers set up the London Lead Mining Company in the 18th century. The Mines Heritage Centre has more information.

The mines and their machinery are silent but the scattered hill farms recall how mining families grew crops to subsidise their meagre wages.

The heather-clad moors, fells and valleys are alive with curlews, lapwings, peewits, peregrines and grouse, while deer and red squirrel roam this natural fastness.

There is some fine cycling across Alston Moor before you get to Nenthead. You can either take the B6277 past Garrigill or take the more direct A689.

PLACES OF INTEREST

Hartside Nursery Garden
On route one mile from Alston: rare and unusual alpine plants.

The Hub
Station Unit (Opposite rail station), Alston.
Local history museum with eclectic mix. Entry by donation, run by volunteers.
✆ 01434 382244.

South Tynedale Railway Station
England's highest narrow-gauge track runs along 3.6km of former British Rail track. There is a tea room at the old station. Runs every weekend April – October plus some weekends in December, and daily during August.
✆ 01434 381696
✆ 01434 382828 for talking timetable

ⓘ **Tourist Information Centre,** Town Hall, Front St, ✆ 01434 382244

PLACES TO EAT

Alston Wholefoods
Front Street (next to Angel pub), Alston.
Run by: Sarah Sawyer
This is a workers' co-operative, which stocks delicious local products (and candles), specialising in organic and Fair Trade. Has a range of good beers and wines, gourmet ice creams.
✆ 01434 381588
▭ www. cybermoor.org

Alston House
Now in the hands of seasoned chef, Michael Allchorne (See Page 64).
✆ 01434 38220

Cumberland Hotel
(See Page 64)
✆ 01434 381875
✆ 01434 381928

The Moody Baker
Artisan bakery owned by a workers' co-operative. It specialises in delicious pies, quiches etc and are also the originators of the high-energy Moody Baker Biker Bar
✆ 01434 382003

Cumbrian Pantry
Front Street
Good home baking and friendly welcome.
✆ 01434 381406

Blueberry's
Market Place
Good meals, snacks and afternoon tea.

Victoria Inn
Front Street, CA9 3SE
Run by: Steve & Tian Smith

Friendly, family run B&B right in the centre of Alston. Warm, clean and comfortable accommodation offering everything you need. Accepts all major credit cards. Having briefly closed its doors as a pub, the Victoria is now serving again.

- ℓ 01434 381194
- ☞ victoriainncumbria@talk21.com
- 🛏 4S, 2D, 2F
- 💰 £23-£30
- 🍴 Eve Meal: Around £6. Good Oriental twist to Tian's cooking.
- 🍴 Pk Lunch: from £3.50

Alston House
Townfoot, Alston, Cumbria, CA9 3RN
Run by: Michael & Carole Allchorne

Attractive hotel run by a chef who took over in late 2006. Michael & Carole have long experience in the catering business and have great plans for this comfortable, contemporary and stylish setting. Roaring fires in the winter.

- ℓ 01434 382200
- 💻 www.alstonhouse.co.uk
- ☞ info@alstonhouse.co.uk
- 🛏 1D, 3T, 1F
- 💰 £30-£60
- 🍴 Eve Meal: 6-9pm £8-£18
- 🚲 Dist to C2C: On route
- Ⴌ Fully licensed

The Cumberland Hotel
Townfoot, Alston, Cumbria CA9 3HX
Run by: Guy & Helen Harmer

All rooms en-suite, bike storage, drying/cleaning facilities. Only stamping point in Alston. Choice of traditional cask ales and home cooked food. Family run.

- ℓ 01434 381875
- 💻 alstoncumberlandhotel.co.uk
- ☞ info@alstoncumberlandhotel.co.uk
- 🛏 2D, 1F, 2tpl
- 💰 £30-£35
- 🍴 Eve Meal: £6-£15
- 🍴 Pk Lunch: £4.50

YHA Alston
The Firs, Alston,
Cumbria CA9 3RW
Run by: Phil Webster

A 30-bed Youth Hostel provides 3 star affordable dormitory accommodation in the heart of Alston. All bed linen and towels provided. Hot showers and excel-lent washing and drying facilities. Superb selection of meals or self-catering option. Open all year round.

- ℓ 01434 381509
- 📠 01434 382401
- 💻 www.yha.org.uk
- ☞ alston@yha.org.uk
- 🛏 2x2, 2x4, 3x6 (bunks)
- 💰 From £13.95
- 🍴 Breakfast- £4.50 trad English
- 🍴 Eve Meal: £9 for 3 courses
- 🍴 Pk Lunch: £4 or £5.10
- ⓘ Secure cycle storage
- 🚲 Dist to C2C: On route
- Ⴌ Nr pub: 5 minute walk

Lowbyer Manor Country House

Hexham Road, Alston, Cumbria, CA9 3JX
Run by: Richard & Laura Elston

A grade II listed Georgian manor house in the heart of a UNESCO Area of Outstanding Natural Beauty. The C2C passes close by, as do several circular routes around the Alston area, making it an ideal base to explore this corner of Cumbria.

☎ 01434 381230
🖥 www.lowbyer.com
✉ stay@lowbyer.com
🛏 1S, 5D, 2T, 1F
💷 £33-£55

🍴 Pk Lunch: £5
🚲 Distance to C2C: Under 1km. Same for pub.
ⓘ AA 4 star guest house
ⓘ Secure cycle storage and drying facilities

Alston Training & Adventure Centre

High Plains Lodge, Alston, Cumbria CA9 3DD.
Run by: Dave Simpson

Ideal for campers or group bookings, though Alston Adventure Centre will accommodate individuals or small groups under the right circumstances. This is the ideal half-way stopping place, overlooking the Alston Valley with stunning views. Warm comfortable dormitories, lashings of food, and a superb cooked breakfast. Self-catering or camping options also available.

☎ 01434 381886
🖥 www.alstontraining.co.uk
✉ alstontraining@btconnect.com

🛏 10 sleeping 3 or more with total of 45 beds. 2 en-suite shower rooms
🛏 £12 (bedding extra £4)
🍴 Breakfast: £5.50
🍴 Eve Meal: £8.50
🍴 Pk Lunch: £3.50
💷 Camping: £4
🚲 Dist to C2C: 1.5 miles on Nenthead-Garrigill road. 1 mile off-road

Deneholme

Allendale, NE47 9PX
Run by: Sue Mills & Andy Crossan

Luxury 3-star group accommodation in an elegant Edwardian manor house on the edge of Allendale. It is about a seven mile detour, but takes you into an area of outstanding natural beauty, and you can rejoin the route either by crossing Hexamshire Common (for the hardy) or with a trundle down the B6295 to Allenheads, though you might want to stay more than one night. There is an in-house chef, Christine Hutchinson. Minimum number: 12.

Owned by the Fawside charity, which is involved in community regeneration.

☎ 01434 618579
🖥 www.deneholme.co.uk
✉ info@deneholme.co.uk
🛏 5T, 3S, 1D, 2F
💷 20+: £35; 15-20: £40; 12-15: £45
💷 Add £10.50 for dinner
🚲 Dist to C2C: 7 miles
ⓘ Secure lock up. Great for groups
🍺 Pubs nearby

Garrigill

Now a village of some 200 souls, it once had a thriving population of 1,000 thanks to the lead mining. It is a lovely, sleepy village, complete with green, pub and post office. Some of the hardest riding is ahead, so for many it makes a natural overnight stop-off, especially if you have slogged all the way from the fells west of Penrith.

For those who like an extra challenge there is the tough route out of the village, up the very steep and rough track onto the B6277, then left onto a forest track and down into Nenthead the hard way.

The George & Dragon, if it's open, is a good place to refresh the parts that most beers reach. However it has frequently been closed, often doesn't serve food and at the time of going to press was up for sale. Change is likely to mark improvement.

Eastview

Garrigill, nr Alston, Cumbria CA9 3DU
Run by: Lana Dixie

300 year old miner's cottage on the edge of the village green. Immaculate and very comfortable little establishment. TV, DVDs, games, books and maps. Lock-up and drying.

- (01434 381561
- eastview-garrigill.co.uk
- info@eastview-garrigill.co.uk
- 1D, 1T or 1D.
- £25
- Eve Meal: Please give prior notice
- Pk Lunch: £4.50
- Dist to C2C: On it.
- Nr pub: 100m

Bridge View

Garrigill, CA9 3DU
Run by: Margaret Rzas

Comfortable and cosy cottage overlooking the green, just across from the pub. Happy to take cyclists travelling alone. This small friendly B&B sleeps up to three people and the room has tea & coffee making facilities and a colour television. Guests have their own private bathroom.

There is also a secure storage area outside for cycles. Laundry facilities if required.

- (01434 382448
- www.bridgeview.org.uk
- margrzas@cybermoor.org.uk
- 1D/ 1S
- £24
- Pk Lunch: From £4

Village Hall

Garrigill
Run by: Debbie McLauchlan

Just as it says: a village hall. Space for sleeping, though the old mattresses donated by the fire service for communal use have now gone, so bring your own mat. There's also a campsite round the back. £7 a night for the hall, £5 for the campsite (to be paid into a fund jar in the George & Dragon).

- (01434 382 537
- Showers & Kitchen

Nenthead

Folk in both Nenthead and Allenheads – the next port of call – claim to live in England's highest village. I would be interested to know definitively which is the higher. Either way, Nenthead is 500m above sea level and has a colder climate than Aberdeen. It seems incredible that only 300 million years ago it was on the equator.

The village was purpose-built for mining in 1825 by the Quaker Lead Company. In addition to housing they provided a reading room, wash-house, public baths and a school for the 1500 employees in the Methodist stronghold. At weekends they ran smallholdings and this way of life lasted for more than 100 years. A decorative fountain serves as a memorial to RW Bainbridge, superintendent of the mine company.

Falling markets ruined the community, with cheap imports leading to a collapse in prices, and many families emigrated to the USA and Australia at the end of the 19th century. Zinc mining continued until the 1940s and the last pit closed in 1961.

PLACE TO EAT

The Miner's Arms
Serves both draught beer and solid sustenance. You can get an evening meal for around a tenner.

PLACES TO SEE

The Nenthead Mines Heritage Centre
This is a must. They have brought to life the old workings on this 200 acre site and have helped breath life into a village that history managed to forget. You can even do some mineral panning and visit the sites on self-guided trails.
℘ 01434 382294

Killhope Lead Mining Centre
Off the A689 5km east of Nenthead. Underground visits April - October.
℘ 01388 537505.

CYCLE REPAIRS

Mark Fearn
The village blacksmith also repairs bikes, stocks spares and will do a breakdown and recovery service if needed
℘ 01434 382194
📱 07776 098915
✉ mark@fearn2620.freeserve.co.uk
🖥 www.markfearn.co.uk.

Mill Cottage Bunkhouse

Nenthead, Alston, Cumbria CA9 3PD
Run by: Tim Haldon

Assay House and Mill Cottage bunkhouses are part of the Nenthead Mines Heritage Centre. Assay House sleeps up to 12 and has a kitchen diner. Mill Cottage sleeps six in beds styled like bunks in a ship's cabin, with curtains for privacy plus a small internal light and shelf. Both are available for group bookings and there is a cafe on site and a pub in the village. The centre is a scheduled ancient monument marking one of the largest lead and silver mining and processing areas in the country during the 19th century.

✆ 01434 382 726 / 382 037
📠 01434 382 043
💻 www.npht.com
📧 bunkhouse@npht.com
🛏 18
💷 £12 pppn
🚲 Dist to C2C: On route.
🍺 Pub nearby
🍽 Pk Lunch: No
ℹ️ Drying facilities and secure lock-up

Avesgarth B&B

13 Hillersdon Terrace, Nenthead, Alston, CA9 3PG
Run by: Joan Aves

Family run B&B right on the route with secure cycle store and open all year.

✆ 01434 382 656

💻 avesgarth.mysite.wanadoo-members.co.uk
📧 joan@aves.freeserve.co.uk
🛏 1S, 1D 1T, 1F.
💷 £20. U-12s half-price.
🍽 Pk Lunch: £3.75
🚲 Dist to C2C: On route.
🍺 Nr pub: 3mins

Nent Hall Country House Hotel & Farmhouse B&B

Nent Hall, CA9 3LQ
Run by: Helen Patterson

This splendid setting just off the A689 Alston to Nenthead road, about 1.5 miles west of Nenthead. There are some great online deals at the hotel, whilst there are five double rooms across the lane at the Farmhouse B&B. Cycle friendly and stylish, good looking at real prices and affordable country house accommodation.

✆ 01434 381584
💻 www.nenthall.com
📧 info@nenthall.com
🛏 Farmhouse: 3D, 1 family suite (up to 6),
🛏 Hotel: 2D, 3T, 6 four poster, 2 superior 4-poster, and a five room suite
💷 £35 for the farmhouse
💷 £34.50 for the hotel: (But also see the online deals)
🍽 Eve Meal: Bar: from £8–£15. Restaurant: 3 courses from £25.
🍽 Pk Lunch: By arrangement

YHA Ninebanks, *Orchard House, Mohope, Ninebanks, Hexham, NE47 8DQ.*

Six miles from Coalcleugh and seven from Alston. Ninebanks is in former lead miners' cottages now available to non YHA members. Self-catering. Licensed premises. Full catering service for pre-booked groups.

✆ 01434 345288   💻 www.yha.ninebanks.co.uk   📧 ninebanks@yha.org.uk

Allenheads

This is an unremitting stretch with the steepest climb directly out of Nenthead, so if you are staying overnight avoid one of those typically generous Cumbrian breakfasts.

Turn left off the A689 after just over a kilometre of hellish gradient, past the disused lead mineshafts (pictured), and soon you will be crossing the highest point on the route – Black Hill. At 609 metres (just a tad under 2000 feet) it is 29 metres (nearly 100 feet) higher than Hartside . Once you have conquered the climb past Killhope Law it's plain sailing to Allenheads.

This is a delightful village nesting among the trees. Its focal point is a marvellous little pub called the Allenheads Inn where a cornucopia of fascinating nick knacks are suspended from ceilings and walls, doors and passageways.

A century ago this prosperous, peaceful little haven was a toneless grey valley of slag heaps shrouded by smog, a mining community that provided one sixth of the nation's lead. It slipped into decline along with the industry but has revitalised itself, and there is now a Trust, a visitor centre, mining exhibitions, a shop and a café.

It is also home to the British Norwegian Ski Club. There are three tow ropes on the run to the top at 540 metres. Annual family membership is £30. Facilities on the piste include a small bait hut where there is a BYO glühwein facility. Apres ski is in the pub.

An ideal place for celebrities, it is usually free of paparazzi and gossip columnists. A popular haunt with the beau monde of Carlisle and Newcastle, Allenheads is again a coming place.

PLACES OF INTEREST

Woodland Nature Trail
Walks that take you around the village.

Old Blacksmith's Shop
Smithy with display.

The Allenheads Trust
Allenheads Heritage Centre
℡ 01434 685043

Thorn Green Accommodation
Thorn Green, Allenheads, Hexham NE47 9JQ
Run by: Julie Macdonald

Bunkhouse, campsite and holiday cottage right on C2C about a mile before Allenheads. Bunkhouse has seating area and television plus drying room. Locked bike shed holds 12 bikes. The Allenheads Inn just up the road provides evening meals.

℡ 01434 685234
📱 07977 728328
✉ hammershields@btopenworld.com

- 🛏 2–6 Bunks Each + 2 Showers
- 💷 £18 pppn
- 🍴 Pk Lunch: Please give a day or so advance warning
- 🚲 Dist to C2C: On route
- 🍺 Pub nearby
- ℹ Drying facilities and secure lock-up

The Allenheads Inn

Allenheads, nr Hexham, Northumberland NE47 9HJ

Run by: Ann & Phil Homer

18th century village inn renowned reputation. A must for many cyclists who enjoy atmosphere, hospitality and all-round comfort. Fine ales and big helpings of tasty food. Camra & Good Pub Guide. Single occupancy restricted during the busy season.

- ☎ 01434 685 200
- 🖥 www.theallenheadsinn.co.uk
- ✉ philann@phomer.fsbusiness.co.uk
- 🛏 1D,4T,2F
- 💷 £27-£31

- 🍽 Eve Meal: Main courses £7.50
- 🍽 Pk Lunch: £4.50
- 🚲 Dist to C2C: On route

Allenheads Lodge

Allenheads, Northumberland, NE47 9HW

Central heating, secure bike lockup, drying room, separate showers.

- ☎ 0191 564 0291
- ✉ allenheadslodge@springboard-ne.org
- 🖥 www.springboard-ne.org
- 🛏 4 (Total of 22 beds)
- 💷 £20.50
- 🍽 Pk Lunch: £4.50
- 🍽 Eve Meal: On Request
- 🚲 Dist to C2C: On route
- 🍺 Nr pub: 700m

New Houses

Allenheads, Northumberland NE47 9HX

Run by: Pat & Terry McMullon

Warm, spacious and very comfortable cottage with all amenities. Walking distance to pub.

- ☎ 01434 685 260
- ✉ zookon@aol.com
- 🛏 1S, 2T
- 💷 £20-£30
- 🍽 Pk Lunch: From £3.50
- 🚲 Dist to C2C: On route
- ⓘ Drying facilities & secure lock-up

Hemmel Cafe

Allenheads

Run by: Jacquie Robson

Somewhere between a cafe and a restaurant serving wine, coffee and tea, Jacquie's home cooking offers up dishes from chicken and pasta bake to steak pie and all-day breakfast. Vanilla

sponges and home baked cakes jostle for space in this charming converted cattle byre with its airy courtyard tucked away behind the car park.

- ☎ 01434 685568
- 🖥 www.thehemmel.com
- ✉ jacquie.robson@btinternet.co.uk
- 🍽 Eve meal: £5.50-£8.50

Ordnance Survey © Crown copyright: 100039985

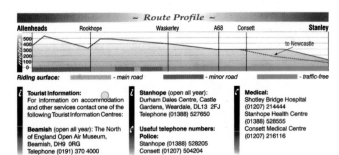

Tourist Information:
For information on accommodation and other services contact one of the following Tourist Information Centres:

Beamish (open all year): The North of England Open Air Museum, Beamish, DH9 0RG
Telephone (0191) 370 4000

Stanhope (open all year):
Durham Dales Centre, Castle Gardens, Weardale, DL13 2FJ
Telephone (01388) 527650

Useful telephone numbers:
Police:
Stanhope (01388) 528205
Consett (01207) 504204

Medical:
Shotley Bridge Hospital
(01207) 214444
Stanhope Health Centre
(01388) 528555
Consett Medical Centre
(01207) 216116

Rookhope

The stretch out of Allenheads is almost the last tortuous ascent – but it does seem to drag on to the summit at Currick. Then there is a nice stretch of gentle downhill to Rookhope.

You soon pass the boundary into County Durham, land of the Prince Bishops – palatinate rulers with absolute authority equal to a sovereign within their area. They were granted such power because of the strategic importance of the area in the ongoing battle with the Scots.

You will pass the Lintzgarth Arch (pictured opposite), an incongruous vestige of a bygone era lying abandoned on the valley floor. It carried a 3km horizontal chimney which replaced the conventional vertical type when it was realised that a lot of lead literally went up in the smoke. Teams of sweeps were employed to scrape the valuable lead and silver deposits from the

chimney once a week. It was a dangerous and filthy job, and so done by children.

Rookhope is another shrunken mining village. It is also charming, well guarded from sight high above the Weardale Valley. It is hard to imagine that this small haven was a hive of activity only a few years ago. In its heyday it supported a surgery, a resident district nurse, vicar, policeman, teashops, several crowded pubs and a busy school. The mining of lead, iron and fluorspar, smelting and the railways totally dominated people's lives.

Today the village is a welcome watering hole and resting place for weary cyclists before the final leg of the C2C journey down to the NE coast. Now there is only a pub (newly refurbished), village shop, post office and working man's club – but a splendid stopping off point, nonetheless.

The Old Vicarage
1 Stotsfield Burn, DL13 2AF
Run by: Colin & Pauline Lomas

Detached stone-built house in secluded grounds with an orchard garden and courtyard. Large lounge, log fire, TV/Video/DVD and board games. You can stroll to the pub and enjoy real ales in a convivial atmosphere.

The grounds accommodate tents in a simple and tranquil location with a wc, h/c hand basin and shower plus separate sinks for washing-up etc. Camping is £5.00 pp

per night. Please book in advance.

📞 01388 517375
📠 01388 517701
📧 colin@finetime.wanadoo.co.uk
🛏 1Tpl, 2Q
💷 from £27.50
🍽 Pk Lunch: £3.50
🍽 Eve Meal: £9.50 (vegetarian option)
🚲 Dist to C2C: On route

The Rookhope Inn
Rookhope, Weardale, Co. Durham DL13 2BG
Run by: Tom & Alex Goundry

Cycle friendly and geared to your needs, not least in the shape of the beers available ... there's a frequently changed selection of real ale incluing the likes of Green King and Black Sheep. The Rookhope Inn is in the CAMRA Good Beer Guide. A range of traditional dishes are always available, using locally sourced ingredients wherever possible. Delightful setting and great fun place to be.

☎ 01388 517 215

🖥 www.rookhope.com
✉ checkin@rookhope.com
🛏 4T, 1F (all en-suite)
💷 £30
🍽 Pk Lunch: £4.50
🍽 Eve meal & lunch: Snacks to full a la carte. Vegetarian options.

Eastgate

> To get to Eastgate for those heading towards Hole House Bunkhouse and the comforts of the Cross Keys, take Route 7 signs for Stanhope. Just outside Rookhope you will see that the C2C branches off to the left: ignore, and continue straight on, soon crossing the Rookhope Burn. It's a couple of miles down to the village and then a couple of miles east to Stanhope, where you rejoin the official route. As accommodation in this wonderfully remote part of the world is limited, the addition of Hole House is indeed welcome.

Hole House Bunkhouse B&B
Hole House, Weardale DL13 2HX
Run by: Nick & Lorraine Thwaites

Charmingly converted bunkhouse on a farm in the village of Eastgate between Rookhope and Stanhope. Ideal for cyclists and walkers and very reasonably priced. Secure lock-up for bikes.

☎ 01388 517184
✉ holehousebunks@btinternet.com
🛏 3Q

💷 £18.50 (bunk bed)
🍽 Eve Meal: Local pub 600m away
🍽 Pk Lunch: By arrangement
ⓘ Drying facilities
ⓘ Secure lock-up

Allenheads–Rowlands Gill/Stanley

73

Stanhope

From Rookhope you can take the exciting but demanding off-road section which climbs steeply past ruins and heads along the edge of Edmundbyers Common, leading down to the Waskerley Way either by road or across a track – the choice is yours.

The second choice is to go via Stanhope, one of Weardale's more important and historic little market towns. But if you go this way, remember that you'll be facing a swine of a climb up the B6278 to the Waskerley Way, aptly called Crawley Side.

ABOUT THE AREA
Sleepy backwater that reaped the rail reward

Originally a Bronze Age settlement on the banks of the River Wear, then a tiny village clustered around its cobbled market square. Then Stanhope & Tyne Railway was built to take industrial produce to Consett and Cleveland along the Waskerley Way and suddenly it was bustling.

Before the railway, all raw materials had to be transported by pack horses. Teams of tough Galloways would pick their way over the Pennines and then down into the valleys, the lead horse often having a bell on its harness to guide the following horses across the mist-cloaked moors.

EATING OUT

The Bike Stop
Stamping post that also serves great teas. You'll find it at mile post 100 (also see the cycle shops section).

THINGS TO DO

Durham Dales Centre & Castle Gardens
Good café, information centre and craft shops.
- 🖳 www.durhamdalescentre.co.uk
- ✆ 01388 527 650

St Thomas's Church
12th century origins complete with Roman altar and Saxon font. In the grounds is the 350-million year old fossilised tree found in 1914 in an Edmundbyers mine.

Queens Head Hotel
89 Front Street, Stanhope, Weardale, DL13 2UB
Run by: John Emerson & Carol Patillo
Hotel has public bar. A small, friendly local pub with bar and dining room, stocking a good pint of real ale.

- ✆ 01388 528 160

- 🖳 www.queenshead stanhope.co.uk
- ✉ info@queenshead stanhope.co.uk
- 🛏 4T
- 💷 £25-£30
- 🍽 Pk Lunch: About £5
- 🍽 Eve Meal: £3-£7 (7-8pm)

Belle Vue Farm

Hall Road, Stanhope, Weardale. DL13 2EZ
Run by: Howard & Linda Lazenby

Howard and Linda created Belle Vue Farm Cottages as a haven for those who love the peaceful and restful environment with its panoramic views. The attention to detail creates a warm and welcoming atmosphere in private detached cottage-style accommodation. There is a secure cycle store and guests may service and wash their bicycles at the workshop. Continental breakfast. No children under 14 years or pets. Private fishing pond.

- (01388 526225
- www.tranquil-life.info
- relax@tranquil-life.info
- 4D, 1T all en-suite
- From £62 to £72 per room
- (i) Secure cycle storage
- Dist to C2C: Close to Stanhope branch
- Nr pub: ¾mile
- (i) Open all year round

Jubilee Adventure Centre

Crawleyside, Weardale.
Run by: Nadine Kipling

In the beautiful village of Crawleyside just above Stanhope. (Advert: Page142)

- (01388 463712
- 42 beds.
- £3.50 (bed only)
- Self catering kitchen and dining room (includes crockery)

Parkhead Station

Stanhope Moor, DL13 2ES
Run by: Terry & Lorraine Turnbull

A licensed B&B with tea room on the 100 mile marker, three miles north of Stanhope on the Waskerley Way. In an AONB with beautiful panoramic views and downhill all the way (almost) to the coast. Drying facilities and secure lock-up. Take a virtual tour on the website.

- (01388 526434
- www.parkheadstation.co.uk
- parkheadstation@aol.com
- 2D, 2F plus The Sleeper (up to six)
- from £25
- Eve Meal: Available, but must pre-order
- Pk Lunch: £3.50
- Licensed
- Dist to C2C: On route
- (i) VisitBritain: 3 stars

CYCLE SHOP

The Bike Shop

Run by Terry & Lorraine Turnbull at Mile Post 100, which you find at the start of the Waskerley Way, 5km from Stanhope.
ß 01388 526434

Stanhope also has a historic church

Edmundbyers & Castleside

Edmundbyers is a popular stopping off point. To get to it, continue along the B6278 instead of turning right for the Waskerley Way. It is buried amongst the heather and wild moorland of Muggleswick Common and is close to the wonderfully picturesque village of Blanchland.

Many cyclists continue along the B6278 to Shotley Bridge, bypassing Consett and linking up with the C2C just beyond. If Edmundbyers were to be on the Sustrans map, it would be underneath the superimposed panel showing Consett's town centre.

For those who don't feel like self-catering in the kitchens of the YHA, there is the Punch Bowl pub in the centre of the village, which does evening meals.

Edmundbyers YHA

Low House, Muggleswick Common, Consett, DH8 9NL

This hostel is a former inn dating from 1600 with beamed ceilings and a cosy open fire, and has been refurbished to provide a comfortable and memorable place to stay. The village of Edmundbyers is surrounded by a 360-degree panorama in a heather moorland area of outstanding natural beauty. Only quarter of a mile from Derwent Reservoir, which is ideal for watersports and trout fishing.

- 📞 01207 255651 or 0870 7705810
- 🖥 www.yha.org.uk
- ✉ edmundbyers@yha.org.uk
- 🛏 1Tpl, 1Q, 2 dorms for 5, 2 dorms for 6.
- 💷 from £15.95 (from £11.95 for U18s)
- ℹ Self-catering . Shop on site
- 🍽 Meals: Pub nearby

Bee Cottage is one of the favoured watering holes of seasoned C2Cers and lies on a bend in the Waskerley Way just beyond Park Head Plantation. It is on the edge of a pretty little coppice and a couple of miles before the A68 at Castleside.

Bee Cottage Guesthouse

Castleside, DH8 9HW

Run by: David Blackburn & Irene Mordey

Stunning views. Quiet rural setting. All en-suite. Clean, comfortable accommodation. Warm welcome guaranteed. Member of Walkers & Cyclists Welcome schemes.

Leave the C2C at Redhouse Farm on the Waskerley Way.
- 📞 01207 508 224
- 🖥 www.beecottage.co.uk
- ✉ beecottage68@aol.com
- 🛏 2D, 2twn, 4f

- 💷 £35–£45
- 🍽 Pk Lunch: £6
- 🍽 Eve Meal: (please give advance warning). £20 (3 Courses + coffee & mints)
- 🚲 Dist to C2C: On route.
- 🍸 Pub nearby
- ℹ Visit Britain 4 Star. Cyclists Welcome Scheme

Consett

Whether you are coming via Edmunbyers Common or Stanhope, you will shortly be passing the 100 mile point stamping station at the Bike Stop at the start of the Waskerley Way.

You can get spares and repairs here, or tea and cake. And it's down hill the rest of the way. This is a pleasant and easy section of the route, past Muggleswick Common, Waskerley and Smiddy Shaw reservoirs, followed by a quick canter into Park Head Plantation near Bee Cottage, and down to the A68. You pass the magnificent Hownsgill Viaduct which carried the Stanhope and Tyne Railway Line, Britain's first commercial railway. There are great views across sweeping tracts of forest and undulating landscape, on the edge of an area that was once the embodiment of heavy British industry.

The pathway is dotted with imaginative Sustrans signage and sculptures cast from industrial relics. Before Consett are the Terris Novalis sculptures, which overlook the 700 acre site of what was once the mighty Consett Steelworks. The Turner prize winning works – a stainless steel theodolite and an engineer's level by Tony Cragg, (pictured next page) – are nearly 7m tall, are 20 times life size, and symbolise regeneration in an area convulsed by the death of heavy industry late last century. The works were commissioned by Sustrans and will stand as a monument to this admirable body long after the combustion engine has had its day.

"The work sited at Consett marks the watershed between the upland/moorland landscape and the extremes of the Industrial Age," says the Sustrans website.

DIRECTIONS

As you enter Consett, you have a decision to make. The routes part company here; one goes to Sunderland (top on the map, right) and the other to Newcastle (left on the map).

The original route took riders into Sunderland, so I shall deal with this one first.

🚲 Head for **Stanley**, paying heed to the signs as you exit Consett. Round the A692 roundabout, briefly up the left side

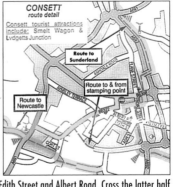

CONSETT route detail

Consett tourist attractions include: Smelt Wagon & Lydgetts Junction

Route to Sunderland

Route to & from stamping point

Route to Newcastle

of Front Street before going left between Edith Street and Albert Road. Cross the latter half way up and go right into Park Road, cross Front Street before heading left and across the B6308, then the path takes you through Leadgate and past the Annfield Plain. Look out for the Kyo Undercurrents sculpture – a series of earth and stone ramps.

🚲 If you are heading for **Newcastle**, you turn left just after the Hownsgill Viaduct, and skirt to the west of Consett town centre, cross both the A692 and A691 following the route heading northeast to **Rowlands Gill**. (This route resumes: Page 92)

The Bike Bus
The Bus Station, Stanley, Co Durham DH9 0TD
Cyclist and bike transport specialists. Operates throughout the UK and size of group no object. Very competitive rates. For more details, see advert on back cover.
- 01207 237424
- www.stanleytaxis.co.uk
- bike.bus@btconnect.com

Hownsgill Bunkhouse
Hownsgill Farm, Consett, DH8 9AA
Run by: John & Stephen Shaw

Situated on the Lydgetts Junction, between the wonderful Hownsgill Viaduct and the Consett section of the Stanhope to Tyne former rail track and Sculpture Trail.

- 01207 503597 or 07946 797278
- www.c2cstopoff.co.uk
- hownsgill_bunkhouse@hotmail.co.uk
- from £16 (discounts for u-18s)
- 2 four bed bunks; 1 two bed bunk room; 1D.
- Kitchen diner seats up to 12
- Drying area. Wet room, washing machine/tumble dryer etc
- Patio/barbecue area   Car parking

Deneview
15 Front Street, Castleside, Consett, DH8 9AR
Run by: Catherine O'Keefe

Superior B & B accommodation. Colour digital TV. Radio and Tea/Coffee making facilities. Only 25 yards from an excellent pub serving meals each day. 4 Diamond Award.

- 01207 502925
- www.deneview.co.uk
- catherine@deneview.co.uk
- 1D, 1T, 2S (all en-suite)
- £25–£30
- Open all year
- Secure storage
- Pk lunch: yes
- Eve meal: Pub 25m
- Dist to C2C: ½ mile

Consett YMCA
Pariament St, Co. Durham, DH8 5DH
Run by: Terry Page

There is a drying room, workshop for repairs, colour TV, bar and lounge, pool table, and even a gym if you have the energy left! Accommodates up to 45 people. Also organises outdoor activities. Adventure activities programmes and holidays a speciality.

- 01207 502680
- www.consettymca.org
- ymca@derwentside.org.uk
- 10F
- £15 (or £10 without breakfast)
- Eve Meal: £5
- Pk Lunch: £3

TERRIS NOVALIS

Industrial heritage recalled in sculpture

Crown and Crossed Swords Hotel
Front Street, Shotley Bridge, Consett, Co. Durham, DH8 0HU
Run by: Sheila, Victoria or Maureen

Vibrant pub in the heart of the scenic village of Shotley Bridge, a short hop from the Consett to Rowlands Gill route. Public Bar, Lounge Bar, Restaurant and ten letting bedrooms. Private car park. Old fashioned and lovely — time has stood still here.

- ☎ 01207 502006
- ☎ 01207 583111
- ⌂ 1S, 2D, 4T, 2F (4 en-suite)
- 💷 from £25

- 🍽 Eve Meal: Yes
- 🍽 Pk Lunch: Yes (please order in advance)
- ⓘ Secure cycle storage
- 🚲 Dist to C2C: 500m

Places to visit
Phileas Fogg: *Alias Derwent Valley Foods Factory. You will smell it before you see it.*

Shotley Bridge: *An old spa town, well-known for German swordmakers in the 17th century.*

C2C Features
Dotted along the line are storyboards set on vertical sleepers which interpret the history of the railway. These are chapters taken from a novel, The Celestial Railroad, by John Downie. It is available from Sustrans North Eastern Office at Stanley.
- ☎ 01207 281 259.

Cycle shops
Consett Cycle Co
62 Medomsley Rd
- ☎ 01207 581205

McVickers Sports
Front Street
- ☎ 01207 505121

Eating out
Grey Horse
Real ales brewed on the premises. Light lunches. Right on C2C route.

Jolly Drovers Pub
Leadgate
- ☎ 01207 503 994

MOTECH
62/64 Medomsley Road
- ☎ 01207 581205

Stanley

Stanley is set on a breezy hill top and commands a bird's eye view of the whole area. It is a former mining town situated between Consett and Chester-le-Street, the name comes from Anglo-Saxon and means 'stony field'.

The first written reference to it dates to 1211 but there is evidence that there were earlier settlements in the area with both Neolithic and Roman remains having been discovered. It expanded quickly during the Industrial Revolution but suffered badly after the demise of the mining industry with other big employers also pulling out of the town.

THINGS TO SEE

Beamish Museum
England's largest open-air museum, which features a working steam railway, trams, a Victorian town centre, a demonstration colliery, a school and a working farm. The C2C route passes within yards of the entrance gate.

Tanfield Railway
The oldest railway in the world that still exists. It stops at the Causey Arch north of Stanley — 50m high and a Scheduled Ancient Monument built in 1728 — and is manned by volunteers .
  ℓ 0191 274 2002

Jolly Drovers Maze
Built on the site of the former Eden Pit Colliery in 1989. Like the Lambton Worm (see Chester-le-Street) it was designed by Andy Goldsworthy.

Beamish Mary Inn
No Place, Beamish, Co. Durham DH9 0QH
Run by: Graham Ford
Traditional Inn. Specialises in good food, real ale, live music. Comfortable atmosphere. All rooms en-suite, one with a private bath. Cyclists/walkers most welcome.
  ℓ 0191 370 0237
  ℓ 0191 370 0091
  💻 www.beamishmary.co.uk
  📧 beamishmary@hotmail.com

  ⌁ 4D
  💷 from £25
  🍽 Eve meal: from £4
  ⚙ Dist to C2C: 500m (behind Beamish Museum)

Ordnance Survey © Crown copyright: 100039985

Stanley   Washington   A19(T)   Sunderland

500
400
300
200
100
0

Riding surface: ▬▬▬ - main road   ▬▬▬ - minor road   ▬▬▬ - traf

Tourist Information:
For information on accommodation and other services contact one of the following Tourist Information Centres:

Beamish (open all year):
Beamish Open Air Museum,
Beamish, DH9 0RG
Telephone (0191) 370 4000

Sunderland (open all year):
50 Fawcett Street,
Sunderland, SR1 1RF
Telephone (0191) 553 2000/01/02

Useful telephone numbe
Police:
Chester le Street, Birtley,
Washington & Sunderlan
(0191) 214 6555
Medical:
Washington (0191) 415 1:
Sunderland (0191) 565 6:

DIRECTIONS

Scrap transformed into landmark artworks

Just follow the transformed transformers (great steel monoliths sculpted from reclaimed scraps which have assumed iconic status – the Stanley Sphinxes). Don't forget to look at the metal cows near Beamish. Created by Sally Matthews, they are surprisingly graceful as they stand beside the path, turning grass into rust.

There's also King Coal by artist David Kemp, next to the abandoned railway line at Pelton Fell. This was built of stone from the dismantled Consett railway station bridge, bricks from old kilns and British Coal provided the crown. It was put together by a stonemason and local volunteers and was, by sheer coincidence, finished on October 15 1992 – the very day of the announcement of the closure of the last pits in Durham coalfields.

Chester-le-Street is the oldest town in County Durham, and was once a Roman settlement. The Washington Wildfowl and Wetlands Centre is very near the route. This 100-acre waterfowl park designed by Peter Scott has over 1,200 birds and is visited by several mammals including the scarce water vole.

Chester-le-Street

THE LAMBTON WORM

If you manage to leave the river here in one piece, be thankful! For this is where the Lambton Worm resides (and we are not referring here to the erstwhile politician).

The legend runs that a young Lambton lad, fishing in the river against all advice, caught a small worm. In disgust he threw it into a nearby well and went off to fight in the Crusades.

On his return the "worm" had grown into a dragon which ravaged the countryside. A witch agreed to slay the beast on condition that Lambton kill the first living thing he met. Unfortunately it was his father, whom of course he spared, and so failed to fulfil his side of the bargain, thus nine generations of Lambtons were condemned to meet untimely ends.

PLACE TO VISIT

The Washington Wetlands Trust
100 acres of magnificent parkland, ponds and hides on the way to Sunderland.
☎ 0191 416 5454

EATING OUT

The Wheatsheaf
Pelaw Grange
☎ 0191 388 3104

The Barley Mow
Browns Buildings
☎ 0191 410 4504

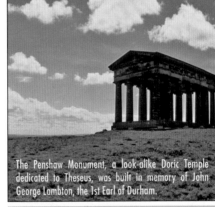

The Penshaw Monument, a look-alike Doric Temple dedicated to Theseus, was built in memory of John George Lambton, the 1st Earl of Durham.

CYCLE SHOP: Cestria Cycles, *11 Ashfield Terrace*
☎ 0191 388 7535

Malling Guest House
1 Oakdale Terrace, Chester-le-Street, DH2 2SU
Run by: Wendy Rippon

Heather's daughter Wendy has taken over this 17-year-old cycle-friendly business, and is putting lots of energy into making things work smoothly. Once a doctor's house with surgery attached, and is warm and friendly, with a couple of really good pubs on the doorstep.

☎ 0191 370 2571
🖳 www.mallingguesthouse.freeserve.co.uk
✉ wendy@kafs.wanadoo.co.uk
🛏 2S, 1T, 1F
💰 £25–£35
🍽 Pk Lunch: £5
🚲 Dist to C2C: 300m
🍺 Pub opposite

Sunderland
DIRECTIONS

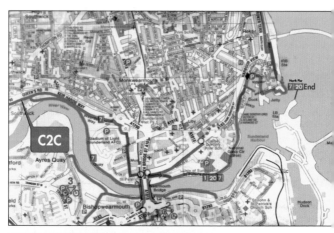

The home run
The last leg of the route is scenic as it follows the north bank of the Wear, skirting Washington and passing the Stadium of Light. This route opened in 2000 and is reasonably easy to follow. The end is at the Marina at Roker, a grand spot to finish. Tradition has it that you dip your wheel in the briny – just as you did at the start.

The River Wear
The River Wear in Sunderland is estuarial, much of it protected for wildlife species and habitat including salt marsh. In the summer it is possible to spot salmon, as well as feeding kittiwakes, common terns, cormorants and herons. Much of the riverside is unrecognisable compared to just 20 years ago when it was dominated by collieries, engineering works and dozens of shipyards.

The C2C heads eastwards under the Leamside railway line, which crosses the River Wear via the Victoria Viaduct, so named because it was completed on the day of Queen Victoria's coronation in 1838. The elegant design is based upon a Roman viaduct at Alacantra in Spain.

ABOUT THE CITY

Heritage, history and culture at your seaside rendezvous

Sunderland was once home of shipbuilding, coal-mining, glass blowing and rope making, but it has reinvented itself since becoming a city in 1992 and is now a fascinating mixture of history, heritage and modern facilities to welcome the rider on the last few miles of their voyage.

It lies alongside the River Wear, and there has been a major trading hub here since Anglo-Saxon times, when it was one of Europe's major centres of learning and education thanks to the twin monastic settlements of St Peter's – built in 674 and with examples of oldest stained glass in England, pictured – and St Paul's. It was there that the Venerable Bede wrote the first history of England and it was also here that the art of glass blowing was introduced.

By the middle ages, it was one of the biggest and wealthiest towns in England, and that was before the real boom times arrived during the Industrial Revolution, when its population exploded from 15,000 to 150,000 in just a few years. That was when the harbour created to handle a few small ship yards catering for the fishing fleet, blossomed to become the biggest international centre for shipbuilding with as many as 16 working yards. Then, in 1988 more than 550 years of history ended when the last yard closed.

The coal trains and the heavy industry are long gone, but the grandeur of those Victorian riches can still be seen in echoes of the shipyards visible from the Wearmouth bridge, the elegant architecture and the country parks at Roker and Mowbray. Now, though, the dockside that was one filled with soot, coal dust and the sparks flying from the yards is now an elegant sculpture trail where tranquillity and works of art have replaced the crash of industry.

Nowadays, it is a city in tune with nature, the country parks at Herrington and Hetton Lyons are worth the diversion and the route skirts the Wildfowl and Wetland Trust nature reserve at Washington, and when you reach the sea, you are greeted by the longest stretch of cityside beach in the UK. It is also reinventing itself as a modern waterfront city with bars, restaurants and a thriving nightlife (if you've got the energy for dancing after pedalling over the spine of England) to welcome you.

On the way you pass Washington village, the ancestral home of George Washington, winner of the American War of Independence: symbolically completing the loop since Whitehaven, the start of the C2C, is where his grandparents had their home.

PLACES TO VISIT

Arts Centre Washington
Biddick Lane, Fatfield District 7,
Washington, Tyne & Wear, NE38 8AB
The Arts Centre Washington is a vibrant focus for arts activities offering a year round programme of arts activities includes exhibitions, theatre, dance, music, festivals, classes and workshops for all ages.

✆ 0191 219 3455

💻 www.artscentrewashington.com

Washington Wildfowl & Wetland Centre
Pattinson, Washington NE38 8LE
This recreated wetland provides a 'stop over' and wintering habitat for migratory waterbirds after their passage over the North Sea and the Wetland Discovery Centre offers both a window on the wide range of wildlife and a programme of art exhibitions.

✆ 0191 416 5454

💻 www.wwt.org.uk

The Sunderland Empire
High Street West, Sunderland SR1 3EX
Opened in 1907, is the North East's largest theatre and a splendid example of Edwardian architecture. Following a £4.5million refurbishment the Empire now boasts 21st Century facilities and is the only theatre between Manchester and Edinburgh capable of staging large West End productions.

✆ 0870 602 1130

💻 www.getlive.co.uk/sunderland

Sunderland Museum & Winter Gardens
Burdon Road, Sunderland SR1 1PP
Sunderland's museum is hugely popular with visitors of all ages and offers a range of fascinating multimedia installations to tell the city's story from its early foundations to the present day and one of the galleries boasts an extensive collection of paintings by LS Lowry.

✆ 0191 553 2323

💻 www.twmuseums.org.uk

National Glass Centre
Liberty Way, Sunderland SR6 0GL
Housed in an innovative glass-roofed building on the north bank of the Wear, the National Glass Centre is a fascinating experience and visitors can explore the full history of glass making in the UK and see cutting-edge examples of the contemporary glass maker's art.

✆ 0191 515 5555

💻 www.nationalglasscentre.com

Marine Activities Centre
North Dock, Roker, Sunderland SR6 0PW
The marina at Roker is Sunderland's main focus for all types of water-based sports and leisure activities and boasts an Italian restaurant with panoramic sea views. It's also near your C2C finishing line.

✆ 0191 514 1847

SIGHTS ON YOUR WAY

Riverside Sculpture Trail

Between the Wearmouth Bridge and the Marina, the promenade offers a connected trail of specially-commissioned artworks in metal and stone that refer back to the city's history and heritage.

Stadium of Light

Magnificent 48,000-seater stadium built on the site of Wearmouth Colliery that closed in 1994. Well worth a visit, tours are available. Alongside is the brand new Olympic standard 50 metre swimming pool, the only one of its kind between Leeds and Edinburgh.

Opposite stadium

Park that was the end point of the first steam locomotive railway in the world- the Hetton Colliery Railway-, 11 miles from Hetton-le-Hole to coal staithes at the River Wear from 1822. The staithes were used until the late 60's.

City Centre

Across the Wearmouth Bridge stands Sunderland City Centre, incorporating great places to eat, drink and shop and includes bike shops, the Central Railway Station and venues well worth a visit:

Wearmouth Bridge

Built in 1796 and seen as a catalyst for the growth of Sunderland. The previous bridge was at Chester-le-Street. There was a pedestrian toll until 1846, and for vehicles until 1885. The adjacent railway bridge opened in 1879 and carries both Metro and conventional rail.

St Peter's Church

East of the Wearmouth Bridge, alongside the C2C and the University is St Peter's church, home to the Venerable Bede until he moved to St Paul's in Jarrow. There is now a walkway and cycleway linking the two, and you may spot the small blue signs for it along the rest of the route.

Sunniside & Sunniside Gardens

Sunniside Gardens is a large area of public open space in the eastern part of the city centre and the surrounding area is emerging as a new cultural quarter with new bars and restaurants and over 100 listed buildings.

Roker Beach and Pier

With its distinctive red and white granite lighthouse, Roker beach provides a wonderful seaside playground and is an ideal place for water sports, with the Marine Activities Centre and other facilities close by.

PLACES TO EAT AND DRINK

There are a number of public houses near the C2C finishing point. The Harbour View, The New Derby, The Cliff, The Queen Vic, the bar of the Roker Hotel and a few others are all within walking distance. The Smugglers, on the promenade at Roker Beach, was voted the top music venue in Sunderland and they have live music most days of the week.

Bar meals are available at most of these pubs. There are also a number of excellent Italians in Little Italy on the promenade and Santini's and Gabrielle's by the Mariott.

For snacks, try the Bungalow Café on the cliff top at Roker. It is a well-known landmark, an old-fashioned cafe in a tiny bungalow. Next to is the famous signpost, marked: "To Beach" (pointing towards the beach), "To Village" (pointing into Roker), "To Bungalow" (pointing to the cafe), and "To Germany" (pointing out to sea).

Seaburn
Shagorika Traditional Indian very good
Priti Raj: Contempory Indian very nice

Deptford
(Over the Queen Alexandra Bridge)

King's Arms
1 Beech St, Hanover Place, SR4 6BU
(off Trimdon St behind the B&Q)
This is worth the diversion as it's one of the best beer pubs in the North East. It's a ten minute walk from the city centre and is close to the university. Regulars include Timothy Taylor Landlord plus a wide choice of guest beers. There are nine handpumps. CAMRA pub of the year 2005, 2006 and regional North East winner. Lots of wood panelling, a small snug and lots of pictures of old Sunderland.
☎ 0191 567 9804

Saltgrass
Hanover Place, SR4 6BY
Quite why two of Sunderland's best ale houses happen to be tucked behind a B&Q south of the Alexandra Bridge is a mystery that will resolve itself after a few pints of Black Sheep or sundry other guest beers. Old fashioned and friendly. Beamed ceilings and lots of old pictures of this historic place. Popular for Sunday lunches.
☎ 0191 565 7229

Roker
Trattoria Due: At the Marina
Roker Hotel Tavistock: Thai and Italian
Throwing Stones: Top quality food at the Glass Centre

The Promenade
1 Queen's Parade, SR6 8DA
Serves Caledonian, Deuchars and Tetley. Seafront pub with excellent views. Serves good pub grub and upstairs there are four single rooms and three twins.
☎ 0191 529 2226

Harbour View
Benedict Rd, SR6 0NL
Good range of beers very well kept. As the pub's name suggests, it has commanding views over the marina and harbour and is a short distance from Roker beach. Specialises in microbreweries from near and far and there's a quiz night Tuesdays and live music on Thursdays.
☎ 0191 567 1402

Sunderland Marriott

Queens Parade, Sunderland, SR68DB

Sunderland's only four star hotel is on the seafront overlooking the sandy beaches at Seaburn, two miles north of the city centre and very convenient for the end of the route. A full-service hotel offering modern, high quality accommodation for business and leisure travellers alike. All bedrooms have en-suite facilities and many have sea views. If you want to finish the ride in style, there's a cocktail bar and a good restaurant, private parking and good leisure facilities. The hotel

has recently undergone a £0.5 million bedroom refurbishment.

- (0191 529 2041
- www.sunderlandmarriott.co.uk
- seaburnmarriotthotel@marriott.com
- from £45

Lemonfield Hotel

Sea Lane, Seaburn, Sunde2rland, SR6 8EE,
Run by: Gary Hunter

Family run 4 Star guesthouse with an good reputation for service and comfort. Parking facilities. Rooms en-suite with colour TV, Tea & Coffee facilities. Sea views available

- (0191 529 3018
- www.lemonfieldhotel.com
- gary@lemonfieldhotel.com
- 3T, 5D, 2S (all en-suite)
- £25
- Dist to C2C: On route
- Secure storage
- Nr pub: 250m
- 4-star

Abingdon Guesthouse

5 St Georges Terrace, Roker,
Sunderland SR6 9LX
Run by: Karen Dawson

Very handy for the end of the route. Quiet residential street just off the sea front with plenty of availability at weekends, though can be busy in the week. There is a secure yard in which to store bikes.

- (0191 514 0689
- www.abindgonguesthouse.co.uk
- karen@abingdonguesthouse.co.uk
- 6T, 6S
- £22-£33
- Lots of pubs and restaurants nearby
- Dist to C2C: On route

Mayfield Guest House

Sea Lane, Seaburn, SR6 8EE.
Run by: Vincent and Judith Richardson

Attractive building overlooking Seaburn Park and the seafront, close to some good bars and restaurants on Seaburn Promenade, only a few

minutes walk. Just 400m away are long stretches of Blue Flag beach.

- (0191 529 3345
- www.themayfieldhotel. co.uk
- enquiries@ themayfieldhotel.co.uk
- 4T, 5D, 1F.
- £19-£24
- City centre: 2 miles
- 3-stars

Balmoral & Terrace Guest Houses

2/3 Roker Terrace, Sunderland. SR6 9NB
Run by: Darren Smith

Prominently situated on Roker Sea-Front, within easy access of all Sunderland's facilities, as is the finishing point for the C2C bike ride. For those wishing to dine locally, there are an array of bars and restaurants close by, including a Chinese and an Italian. A ten minute walk takes you to Seaburn, where you will find an even wider range of food. For the less adventurous, there are seaside fish and chip shops only a stones throw away.

- ℓ 0191 565 9217 or 5650132
- 🖥 www.thebalmoral.supanet.com
- ✉ thebalmoral@supanet.com
- 🛏 16 rooms
- 💷 £18-£23

Tavistock Roker Hotel

Roker Terrace, Roker, Sunderland SR6 9ND

This landmark Victorian hotel, built in 1842, has recently been refurbished. Facilities include two restaurants (an Italian and a Thai/Chinese), a late bar, conference and banqueting facilities for up to 350, and 57 en-suite rooms, many with views of the North Sea. It is ideally located for the end of the C2C and is not far from the city centre.

- ℓ 0191 567 1786
- 🖥 www.tavistockleisure.com
- ✉ info@rokerhotel.co.uk
- 🛏 57
- 🍽 Eve Meal: Yes: two restaurants (see above)
- 🍽 Pk Lunch: By arrangement

BIKE SHOPS:

Cycle World
222 High Street West, Sunderland, SR1 1TZ
ℓ 0191 5658188 or 5141974
🖥 www.cycleworldshop.co.uk

Peter Darke Cycles
1/2 John Street, Sunderland, SR1 1DX
ℓ 0191 5108155
🖥 www.darkecycles.com

Halfords Bike Hut
Unit 3, Trimdon Street, Sunderland, SR4 6DW
ℓ 0191 5140843
🖥 www.halfords.com

Not all the architecture is Victorian

WHAT NEXT?

Up the coast to join the Reivers route back to the west

There is a wonderful eight mile stretch of coastal cycling between Roker and South Shields, going through Whitburn and Marsden.

Known as the Two Rivers Cycleway, this is part of National Route 1, which becomes the Coast and Castles route once across the Tyne, wending a spectacular and beautiful thread up the Northumberland coast and into the Scottish Borders.

It is also the connection between the C2C and Reivers routes, completing the full circle in about 330 miles. This route follows the beautiful beaches on Roker and Seaburn before passing the Souter Lighthouse and

Marsden Rock, descending to the old ferry link. Close to the Shields' ferry are a number of great bars overlooking the active Tyne estuary, including the Alum House and bars around Mill Dam / Custom House.

If you finish in Sunderland but your car or train are from Newcastle, the Two Rivers Cycleway is the obvious route. Once at South Shields you have the option of taking the ferry across or taking the pedestrian and cyclists' tunnel (note: do NOT attempt the car tunnel). Also note: the Metro does not allow bicycles, though mainline trains do.

Reivers Route starts Page 101

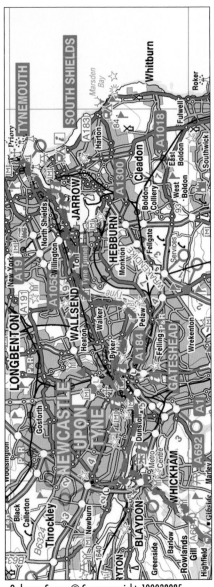

~ Route Profile ~

ds Gill	River Tyne	Newcastle upon Tyne	Wallsend	Tyne Tunnel	**Tynemouth**

surface: ▬▬▬▬ - main road   ▬▬▬▬ - minor road   ▬▬▬▬ - traffic-free

rist Information:
information on accommodation
other services contact one of the
wing Tourist Information Centres:

eshead (open all year):
tral Library, Prince Consort Road,
eshead, NE8 4LN
phone (0191) 477 3339

Newcastle (open all year):
Central Exchange Buildings,
132 Grainger Street,
Newcastle upon Tyne, NE1 5AF
Telephone (0191) 277 8000

Useful telephone numbers:
Police:
Newcastle, North Shields &
South Shields (0191) 214 6555
Medical:
Newcastle General Hospital
(0191) 273 8811
Queen Elizabeth Hospital,
Gateshead (0191) 482 0000

DIRECTIONS

Scenic ride to one of the most happening places in England

The Newcastle route follows the Derwent Walk. This is both scenic and easy to ride, taking you from Rowland's Gill through some landscaped areas alongside the river. When you get to the Tyne go left and over the bridge to the Hadrian's Way path. It starts with a rather unpleasant industrial stretch, but you are soon back beside the river.

The ride along the Quayside is one of the high points. It follows the start of the Coast & Castles route, and the description which follows borrows heavily from my guide book to that magnificent ride from Newcastle to Edinburgh (Coast & Castles - The Complete Guide). I make no apologies.

Newcastle is one of the most `happening' places in northern Europe. A magnet for shoppers and clubbers, diners and drinkers, it boasts some of Britain's finest architecture and has gone through a cultural Renaissance. Recent restoration projects have included Norman fortifications, 16th century merchant houses and the great neo-classical designs of Grainger Town. There are also art galleries, museums and concert venues aplenty. Newcastle and Gateshead, its neighbour on the south bank, have been voted England's best short break destination.

The two towns also teamed up to contend for the European Capital of Culture in 2008, though sadly the gong went to a town arguably in greater need of culture: Liverpool.

Ever since the Romans arrived Newcastle has been a trading hub. It grew up around Pons Aelius, a Roman fortification about 10 miles inland from the North Sea. For the last 800 years a booming trade in wool, leather and coal have brought the city prosperity.

There are now galleries, museums and concert venues, among them the magnificent Baltic Centre for Contemporary Art (pictured). Of 1930s Art Deco design, the redesignation of this former grain warehouse is typical of the vision and flair that has gone into the area's regeneration.

PLACES OF INTEREST

Castle Keep
Castle Garth, St Nicholas St

Built by Henry II between 1168-78 on the site of the so-called New Castle, built in 1080 by William the Conqueror's son, Robert Curthose. The New Castle in turn was constructed on the site of the Roman Pons Aelius (Bridge of Hadrian).

✆ 0191 232 7938

💰 Admission: £1.50, 50p concessions.

The Sage Gateshead

Opened 2005. Sir Norman Foster's contribution to the Geordie quayside, a music complex catering for classical, folk, jazz, brass and choral. This is the home of the Northern Sinfonia.

💻 www.thesagegateshead.org
✆ 0191 443 4661 Ticket Office
✆ 0191 443 4666 Switchboard
✆ 0191 443 4627 Music Education
   Centre Reception
✆ 0191 443 4654 Brasserie Bookings
✆ 0191 443 4634 Coats Desk
✆ 0191 443 4551

BALTIC Centre for Contemporary Art
Gateshead Quays

The major centre for contemporary visual art and stands grandly above the water on the south bank. Five galleries and more than 3,000 square metres. It is housed in an old grain store, part of the old Baltic Flour Mills.

✆ 0191 478 1810

Gateshead Millennium Bridge

This impressive edifice, pictured below, takes walkers and cyclists from Newcastle's Quayside across to Gateshead Quays and Baltic Square and the Baltic contemporary art gallery. The bridge opens and closes like a giant eyelid, allowing shipping to pass. Spectacularly lit at night, like many who inhabit these once louche purlieus, which makes it a great sight after dark.

Grainger Town

A rejuvenated architectural treasure trove with some of Britain's greatest examples of Georgian and Victorian architecture, plus many of the city's top shops.

Chinatown

The name given to the area around Stowell Street. Restaurant standard is good and prices reasonable. Exotic supermarkets and craft shops.

PLACES TO DRINK

Crown Posada, *The Side*
Known locally as The Coffin because it is long and narrow, this is probably the city's best pub. There's no TV, and any music comes either from an old gramophone or the mouths of revellers. There are stained-glass windows, interesting ceilings, wood-clad walls and six excellent ales.
✆ 0191 232 1269

Hotspur, *103 Percy Street*
Popular, single-roomed, city centre pub with four guest ales close to the shopping centre. Busy, and busier still when United are on telly.
✆ 0191 232 4352

The Old George Inn
Cloth Market
One of the 'Toon's' oldest establishments, you reach it down a cobbled back alley. Despite being in the middle of the frantic Bigg Market, where every night is like New Year's Eve, it is a grownup drinking spot.
✆ 0191 269 3061

Duke of Wellington, *High Bridge*
This pub is a one-room wonder, stocking lots of fast changing ales from all over the country. Used to be run by a 50-stone landlord, one of the biggest men in the world, whose bulk would have barred him from entering the Posada.
✆ 0191 261 8852

Bodega, *125 Westgate Road*
According to the Good Beer Guide the highlight of this pub, apart from the range of real ales, is the original twin glass ceiling domes. The pub is a hit with the city's culturati as it stands next to the Tyne Theatre and Opera House. It is a great melting pot as it is also popular with football fans.
✆ 0191 221 1552

Bridge Hotel, *Castle Square*
Big pub looking across at the castle keep. Nestled into the side of the high level bridge. Patio garden at the rear encircled by the old town wall affords great views of the river.
✆ 0191 232 6400

PLACES TO EAT

MODERN

Café 21
*19-21 Queen
St, Quayside*
Simply one of the best restaurants in the north east, you need to book well in advance.
℡ 0191 222 0755

Amer's
*34 Osbourne
Road, Jesmond*
Top place serving good and inexpensive grub means you HAVE to book. Cosy and stylish modern cooking in a trendy spot.
℡ 0191 281 5377

Brasserie Black Door
*The Biscuit Factory,
16 Stoddart Street*
Between Quayside and Jesmond in a 1930s converted factory - the sort of place that is now as voguish as it was hitherto ghastly. Fine cooking in a Modern Art gallery.
℡ 0191 260 5411

Quay 35
35 The Side, Quayside
Early evening 2-course special for £11 or £12. Cosy spot, Quay 35 has a good selection of fish, meat and vegetarian options.
℡ 0191 232 3848

CHINESE

Lau's Buffet King
44-50 Stowell Street
If you want to pack in the protein, this is the place. It's a hugely popular all-you-can-eat that seats 300.
℡ 0191 261 8868

King Neptune
34-36 Stowell Street
Award winning food. Sumptuous surroundings.
℡ 0191 261 6657

INDIAN

Vujon
29 Queen Street
Another classy curry joint. Next to Asha Raval (0191 232 7799) which also comes highly rated.
℡ 0191 221 0601

ITALIAN

La Riveria
Gateshead Quays
℡ 0191 477 7070
Recent addition to Gateshead. Great location and wide choice of Italianate cooking.

Marco Polo
33 Dean Street
Friendly, efficient service. Traditional fare, dim lighting. Marco's is an institution.
℡ 0191 232 5533

Uno's
18 Sandhill, Quayside
Offers a wide range of cheap and cheerful choices. Popular with celebrities.
℡ 0191 261 5264

WORLD FOOD

Kublai Khan
The Side, Quayside
Only place in the area to do Mongolian food. You select your ingredients buffet style and a Mongol Chinese emperor cooks it for you.
℡ 0191 221 1596

Heartbreak Soup
Quayside
Latin American/Mexican/ Central American fare. Eclectic and vibey.
℡ 0191 222 1701

PLACES TO STAY

There are plenty of hotels and guest houses. The Jesmond area, just north of the centre, is full of places to stay and lively night spots. If you're overnighting in the city, there are hotels near the waterfront, down on the fashionable Quayside. For a full list of hotels, call the **Tourist Information Centre:**
℘ 0191 277 8000

Newcastle Gateshead Accommodation Guide
✉ ngi@ngi.org.uk
Newcastle Gateshead Initiative
℘ 0191 243 8800.

Many cyclists enjoy the Quayside area, close to the Central Station. The atmosphere is vibrant, but the hotels, as in most city centres, can be expensive.

Kenilworth Hotel
44 Osborne Rd, Jesmond
Family business run by keen cyclist.
℘ 0191 281 8111
⇝ 12
🛏 £38

The George Hotel
88 Osborne Rd, Jesmond
Small family run concern.
℘ 0191 281 4442
   /2943
⇝ 16
🛏 From £35

Travel Lodge
4 Forster St, Quayside
Family room will sleep three if the double bed is shared.
℘ 0191 261 5432
⇝ 120
🛏 £59.95

DIRECTIONS

Along the banks of the Tyne to journey's end

As you approach the Royal Quays North Sea Ferry Terminus make sure you follow the signs (easily missed) and go to the LEFT of the Wet'n'Wild water centre (you can't miss it – the giant flume tubes look like part of some space-age factory).

Follow the path through landscaped public gardens in which an incongruous cluster of wooden sea groynes stand, as if awaiting tidal erosion. Turn left just beyond them, by a faded waysign – do not head back in the direction of the Amsterdam and Bergen ferry terminal – and go through the modern housing estate. To the right, pleasure craft and fishing boats should be bobbing around at their moorings.

Keep following the C2C, Route 72 and Route 10 signs (they are clustered together) and you will find yourself passing through another modern housing estate. You are now in North Shields, erstwhile home of comedian Stan Laurel.

Following the signs, descend a steep flight of stone steps to the fish quays. You will arrive outside a pub called the Chain Locker, opposite the ferry terminus to South Shields. The view across the Tyne on a good day is worth a pause. You can see, in the far distance, the elegant 19th century façade of the clock tower of South Shields town hall.

Cafes, stores and splendid fish & chip restaurants run the length of the North Shields Quays. This is where Danish and Polish sailors used to integrate vigorously with the local community at a den of iniquity called the Infamous Jungle, now known as the Collingwood Buildings.

You soon round the point where the North Sea meets the Tyne. Welcome to Tynemouth. You pass the 11th century Priory and Castle, and the handsome statue of the man who really won the Battle of Trafalgar in 1805, Admiral Lord Collingwood. Nelson's unassuming and undersung deputy single-handedly took on five French warships for a full hour before the rest of the English fleet caught up. He assumed command upon Nelson's death half-way through the battle, and is Tynemouth's most famous son.

This is a stylish little haven centred upon Front St, a handsome wide avenue built for eating, drinking and promenading. The village is a conservation area of architectural gems from the 18th and 19th centuries. The stretch of shore from here, through Cullercoats and up to Whitley Bay, is known as Newcastle's Côte d'Azur. There is cycle parking in Tynemouth and Whitley Bay, about a mile up the coast.

This is where you finish, though there is no obvious place to crack a bottle of Evian Water. No matter. It is a delightful spot and there is bags of accommodation in Whitley Bay, just round the corner (plus a couple of B&Bs in Tynemouth itself).

Don't forget to dip your front wheel in the water.

Tynemouth is both the end of C2C and start of the Reivers.
For more details about the town see: Page 106

REIVERS
TRAIL

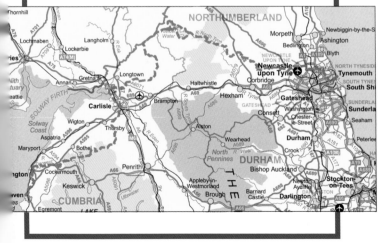

The Reivers route

The Reivers Route opened in 1998 and is 173 miles long. It is also known as the 'Return C2C' as it takes you from the end of the west-to-east route all the way back to the start of the C2C.

It is, however, a great route in its own right — in some ways superior to the C2C — but it has not had as much attention and money spent on it, is not a fully fledged Sustrans route, and has not been given the mile-by-mile care that has been devoted to the C2C over the years. Some are concerned that not enough is being done to push this beautiful and isolated stretch of northern wilderness.

However, the cycle route management unit set up to work closely with local authorities some four years ago along the length of the Reivers, in close co-operation with Sustrans to incorporate the route into the North East Cycle Tourism Strategy, seems to have paid off. The route is reportedly busier than ever.

As with the C2C the gradients along Reivers work in the cyclist's favour. The route winds its way through some of the wildest and most untouched countryside in the UK. It starts at the mouth of the mighty River Tyne, finishes on the Cumbrian coast and along the way, riders follow the shores of Kielder Water — Europe's largest man-made lake — before crossing the Border for a brief foray into Scotland.

Emerging from the post-industrial and partially regenerated suburbs of Newcastle, the route quickly threads its way into the first gentle then rugged countryside of the Northumberland National Park.

There are fine views across to the towering Cheviots before you become immersed in the forest tracks around Keilder, where there are many options suited to mountain bikers and day tripper alike. After the Borders, Carlisle and down through the Lake District.

This is truly isolated terrain. You could be up in the fastnesses of Sutherland or Ross-shire. But unlike up there, you will stumble across such gems as Hesket Newmarket, with its own excellent micro-brewery, Newcastleton just into Scotland, or Cockermouth and Bassenthwaite. There is a lot of satisfaction to be had from such discoveries.

Maps

Though I provide some basic mapping in this book, and there is some waymarking along the way, you should still get the official route map from Footprint (see right).

If you don't mind bulk and cost, the new OS Landranger maps have full route details (though older versions will not have Route 10 marked).

OS Landranger maps: (1:50,000) 88, 87, 80, 79, 86, 85, 90 & 89 (in east to west sequence).

Maps (£4.95) from:

Footprint:
☎ 01786 479866
🖥 www.footprintmaps.co.uk

Sustrans:
☎ 0117 929 0888

Cordee Books & Maps:
☎ 01162 543579
🖥 www.cordee.co.uk

Getting there

The Reivers trail starts at Tynemouth Harbour, a scenic spot looking out to the North Sea with the Priory and Castle the first thing you see when you turn your face inland.

To get there, first head for Newcastle. Then you have the choice of riding out to the starting point along the north bank of the Tyne of if you want to conserve a little energy, there is always the excellent city Metro system.

Aim for Tynemouth station, and when you get there, turn left into Station Terrace and first right into Huntingdon Place. Straight ahead until you join Front Street, which takes you to the coast. Turn right onto Peir Road and head for the car park.

Then let the fun begin.

> Travel details are also included at the start of the C2C guide: Pages 9 & 10

RAIL

There are direct train services from most cities in Britain to Newcastle Central Station. Newcastle is served by Great North Eastern Railways (GNER), Virgin Cross Country and Regional Railways. It takes 2 hours 45 minutes from London, and 1 hour 20 minutes from Edinburgh.

☏ +44 (0)191 221 3156 (station direct line)

To book train seats:

National Rail Enquiry Service
☏ +44 (0)8457 484950
Virgin
☏ +44 (0)8457 222333
GNER
☏ +44 (0)8457 225225

ROAD

Newcastle is easily accessible by car from all parts of the UK. The A1(M) goes through the middle of it. If you are coming by car, there is limited secure parking in the city centre, near Central Station, for between £5.50 and £7 a day.
☏ 0191 243 8294

WAYMARKING

The route is way marked with a blue direction sign complete with the word REIVERS and the route number, 10. These are posted at junctions and other strategic spots. Occasionally the road surface is signed; sometimes there are just little plastic stickers stuck to gates and lamp-posts. Signage is not always brilliant, but with sharp eyes and the use of a map you should not get lost. Having said that, sections at the beginning and end are notorious for lack of signs; vandals like to trash them, and souvenir hunters snaffle them.

Reivers History
TALES OF BLOOD AND GUTS

As you will probably know, the word Reiver means plunderer. The route is named after the murdering bandits who ran a medieval equivalent of Cosa Nostra.

This was the Chicago or Sicily of its time, when marauding clans terrorised both the English and Scottish sides of the Border for 350 years, right up to the 17th century. They lived by cattle rustling, kidnapping, extortion, arson and murder.

The route passes many castles, such as Bew Castle, pictured below, as well as a number of fortified farmhouses, all of which reveal the defensive needs of the area as well as its rich heritage.

Despite the cosy thematising that has been perpetrated by tourism to give the past a false appeal, there is nothing remotely quaint or faintly honourable about Reiving; many of the families were happy to swing both ways, fighting for the English if the price was right, or vice versa.

One family, the Grahams, were so infamous that their surnames were banned by law, so the Grahams changed them to Maharg (Graham backwards), which later also became McHarg.

Indeed, the word 'blackmail' comes from the Reivers: a farmer paid 'blackmail' — rent in the form of cattle instead of the legal 'whiterent', which was paid in silver, to a powerful Reiver who would give him 'protection' in return.

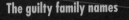

The guilty family names

Archbold; Armstrong; Beattie; Bell; Burns; Carleton; Carlisle; Carnaby; Carrs; Carruthers; Chamberlain; Charlton; Collingwood; Crichtons; Crisp; Croziers; Cuthbert; Dacre; Davidson; Dixon; Dodd; Douglas; Dunne; Elliot; Fenwick; Forster; Graham; Gray; Hall; Hedley; Henderson; Heron; Hetherington; Hume; Irvine; Irving; Johnston; Kerr; Laidlaw; Little; Lowther; Maxwell; Milburn; Musgrove; Nixon; Noble; Ogle; Oliver; Potts; Pringle; Radcliffe; Reade; Ridley; Robson; Routledge; Rutherford; Salkeld; Scott; Selby; Shaftoe; Storey; Simpson; Tait; Taylor; Trotter; Turnbull; Wake; Watson; Wilson; Woodrington; Young.

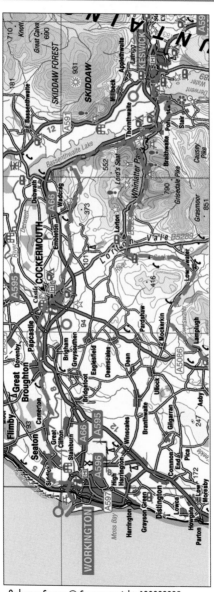

| Tynemouth | | Shiremoor | Backworth | Burradon | Wide Open | Dunnington | **Ponteland** |

```
350
280
210
140
70
0
```

Riding surface: ▭ - main road   ▬ - minor road   ▬ - vehicle track/traffic-free

Tynemouth
ABOUT THE TOWN

The end of the C2C and the start of the Reivers

There are 60s high rise flats and men in cloth caps walking whippets and tending pigeon lofts.

Those of you doing the round trip will recognise the first three miles of the route, since it is the same as the last three miles of the C2C, but at North Shields, it executes a smart right turn and off you go towards the Scottish Border.

There is plenty to do in Tynemouth, which has monuments testifying to a history ranging from Roman times (it is the start of the Hadrian's Wall trail) to the area's recent industrial heritage. Wallsend, nearby, is ideal for the Hadrian's Wall experience. The fort at Segedunum was recently brought back to life at a cost of £9 million, with the only restored Roman bathhouse in Britain.

In medieval times, it was the preferred residence of the queens married to both Edward I and Edward II while their hubbies were off trying to bash the Scots — successfully in the case of the first, less so for his son.

Down river, on the opposite bank, sits Jarrow, home of the Venerable Bede, and the Bede's World Museum. It was also the starting point for the Jarrow March, when 200 protesters descended upon London in 1936 and made one of the most striking political statements in working class history.

Tynemouth Priory and Castle make a spectacular send-off

PLACES TO DRINK

There are several good pubs in Tynemouth. Here are three recommendations:

Tynemouth Lodge Hotel
Tynemouth Road
A real locals' pub frequented by the lifeboatmen. Great beers and often very busy. It's at the top of that steep climb out of the North Shields fish quays, on the edge of Tynemouth. Worth the effort, though, if you have got the energy.

Fitzpatricks
Front Street
A handsome establishment. It is one of eight pubs in the small town. Has a changing selection of hand-pulled ales. Food served.

The Turks Head
Front Street
Otherwise known as the Stuffed Dog because of Willie the Scottish collie, whose 130 year old taxidermised remains sit in a glass box looking at the bar. Willie came down from the Scottish Borders with a herd of sheep and a shepherd, but somehow got separated from them and spent the rest of his life waiting and pining in Tynemouth for his lost master. It is a tale of epic proportions that is told in detail on a plaque. Good Courage Directors, regular guest ales. Food served all day.

PLACES TO EAT

Sidneys
Percy Park Road
Now features in Michelin
☏ 0191 257 8500

Giorgio's Pizzeria & Restaurant
Front Street
☏ 0191 257 3758

Marshall's Fryery at the Priory
Front Street
☏ 0191 257 2435

The Gate of India
40 Front Street
☏ 0191 258 3453

Gibraltar Rock
Carvery East Street
☏ 0191 258 5655

Tynemouth Priory

Whitley Bay

Whitley Bay and Tynemouth adjoin each other so are equally suitable as places to rest before or after your exertions. It is impossible not to notice that this resort, with its Pleasure Dome, Spanish City and seaside villas, is geared up for tourism and little else. Every other building offers food, drink or accommodation — or all three.

In the past Whitley Bay was a thriving holiday resort and it is trying to rediscover its former glory, when smart Geordies would jockey for position on Newcastle Coast's promenade.

York House Hotel

106-110 Park Avenue, Whitley Bay, NE26 1DN

Run by: Michael & Marissa Ruddy

Near start and end of C2C, Reivers and Coast & Castles. 100m to the nearest pub and 250m to the beach. Delightful family run hotel conveniently and yet quietly situated close to all amenities. All rooms are en-suite with fridges and microwaves. Secure indoor cycle storage.

- 0191 252 8313
- 0191 251 3953
- www.yorkhousehotel.com
- reservations@yorkhousehotel.com
- 2S, 5D, 3T, 3F.
- £27.50-£32.50
- Pk Lunch: £5.95
- VisitBritain 4-star (guest accommodation)

Marlborough Hotel

20-21 East Parade, NE26 1AP

Run by: Hilary & Allen Thompson

Sea front family run hotel in prime position. Quality accommodation (the rooms were recently refurbished) and hospitality. Transport links, secure bike parking and drying facilities. Free WiFi throughout.

- 0191 251 3628
- £25-£45
- www.marlborough-hotel.com
- reception@marlborough-hotel.com
- 4S, 6D, 2T, 4F.
- Pk Lunch: £5
- VisitBritain & AA 4 stars

Avalon Hotel

26-28 South Parade, Whitley Bay, Tyne & Wear NE26 2RG

Run by: Michael Farwell

Ideal location: the Avalon is also a pub and is close to the start of Reivers and Coast & Castles, and close to the end of the C2C. Family run 3-star hotel with 16 en-suite rooms, secure bike storage, fully licensed bar, restaurant plus washing and drying facilities. Great breakfast and very cycle friendly.

- 0191 251 0080
- 0191 251 0100
- www.theavalon.co.uk
- info@theavalon.co.uk
- 4S, 4D, 7T, 1F.
- from £35
- Eve Meal: by arrangement
- Pk Lunch: by arrangement

PLACES TO DRINK

Briar Dene
`A former tollhouse with a well-earned reputation for good beer and food,' according to the Good Beer Guide

Fitzgeralds
A half-timbered Victorian pub. Good food and drink as well as being a lively night spot.

Rockcliffe Arms
Attractive one-roomed pub with stained-glass, and two partitioned drinking areas. Proper `locals' pub.

DIRECTIONS

The Footprint map has three large-scale sections showing the best route out of Tynemouth, which I reproduce with their kind permission. There is an alternative route out via Whitley Bay, but the main recommendation is as follows.

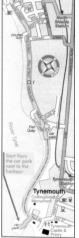

① Start from the car park off Pier Road, facing the Castle and Priory, and take the path along the estuary. Turn left into Cliffords Fort and immediately right into Union Road, then left through the fish quays of North Shields. There may not be so many fishing boats now, but there are many quality fish and chip shops. Union Quay becomes Bell Street, Liddle Street and finally Clive Street.

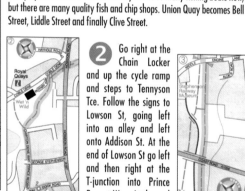

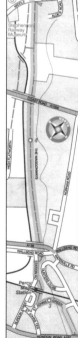

② Go right at the Chain Locker and up the cycle ramp and steps to Tennyson Tce. Follow the signs to Lowson St, going left into an alley and left onto Addison St. At the end of Lowson St go left and then right at the T-junction into Prince Regent Way. At the end of Chirton Dene Way you need to skirt round to the right of the Wet n'Wild tropical indoor water park, with its giant water chutes.

③ Follow the path to the right, along the cycle path parallel with Coble Dene, opposite the huge shopping centre at Royal Quays. This is where the Fjordline and DFDS ferries come in. You now cross Howdon Rd (A187). This brings you to St John's Green. Turn right past Percy Main Station. You will shortly be on the Waggonways, a disused railway line which passes the Stephenson Railway Museum. The famous family hailed from near Wylam, west of Newcastle on the Tyne and the museum has some original locomotives (✆ 0191 200 7145).

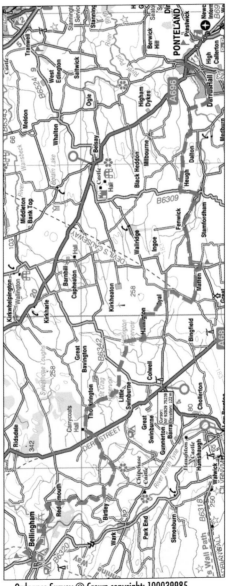

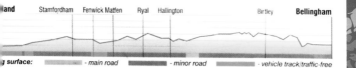

surface: - main road   - minor road   - vehicle track/traffic-free

Stamfordham

DIRECTIONS

Out of the urban sprawl and into the countryside

Once you are past Shiremoor, you are out of the urban sprawl and can settle down to enjoy the countryside.

Go left over the level crossing and through Backworth, Burradon and Seaton Burn, going you past the Big Waters Nature Reserve, Dinnington and up to prosperous Ponteland, where most of the Newcastle United stars live.

After crossing the golf course you arrive in the village at the Diamond Inn. There is a coffee shop to the left and you can lunch at the pub or the Smithy Bistro also immediately on your left, but in reality having covered only 27km, you are unlikely to require much or want to stop for long. If you do take a break, then there are lots of shops, plus pubs and restaurants to be found   here.

Once past Ponteland, you are away from urban life for most of the trip. Go straight across the crossroads but look out for a sign to the right, where you double back on yourself before taking a left hairpin through the smart housing estate of Darras Hall.

At the T-junction at the end of the estate go right, then left towards Donkins House Farm before taking a track up to the right.

This will take you via the back lanes to the lovely village of Stamfordham. This is a handsome and planned estate village with a large green (pictured), a pond and a couple of proper English country pubs, the Bay Horse and the Swinburne Arms.

The church may be Victorian but most of the village is stone-built and 18th century.

The name Stamfordham is Old English for `homestead by the stony ford'. It was once part-owned by Balliol College, Oxford.

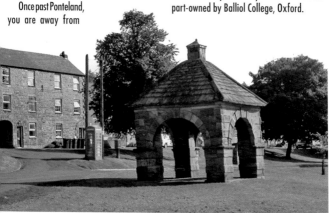

Belsay Hall lies just off the route at Stamfordham

Church House

Stamfordham, Northumberland NE18 0PB
Run by: Mrs Viv Fitzpatrick

Pub adjacent. Pretty village green, old village pubs. 17th-c ivory painted stone house of great character on south side of green. Private residence, good breakfast, welcoming hosts.

- ☎ 01661 886 736
- 📱 07889 312 623
- 📧 bedandbreakfast@stamfordham.
  fsbusiness.co.uk
- 🛏 3 twin
- 💷 £27.50-£35
- 🍽 Pk Lunch: £5
- 🚲 Dist from Reivers: On route

The Bay Horse

Stamfordham, Northumberland, NE18 0PB
Formerly a fortified farm, this inn dates from 1590. Serves good, locally-sourced food and fine ales and offers 21st century comfort in the heart of the village, overlooking the historic green.

- ☎ 01661 886244
- 📞 01661 886940
- 🖥 www.stamfordham-bay.co.uk
- 🛏 5S/T/D, 1F.
- 💷 £27.50-£40 (F £75 and sleeps 5)
- 🍽 Pk Lunch: £4
- 🍽 Eve Meal: £5-£15
- ⓘ VisitBritain 4Stars, 4Diamonds

Wark & Redesmouth

DIRECTIONS

Road to Delight and beyond ...

Head out of Stamfordham keeping the Bay Horse on your left, passing through the hamlet of Fenwick. You will soon be in Matfen, another immaculate estate village. Here take the right turn signed for Ryal and Capheaton, followed by a right-angled left turn just out of the village. It's a couple of km past the hamlet of Delight until you reach the spendidly named Click `em in Farm where you bear right to Ryal.

Just beyond Ryal South Farm there is a track off to the right: if you fancy the off-road option, take it up to Hallington New House, where it joins the road again leading to the cross-roads outside Hallington. Turn right. You can, of course, ignore the off-raod

section, and continue to Hallington along the road.

One km outside Hallington there is another off-road option to the left, taking you across a rough farm track and past the reservoir. Be warned — this track can get pretty muddy. This takes you via Little Swinburn and back onto the main route just before Colt Reservoir.

After a quick left-right shimmy to cross the A68, you will soon pass the edge of Birtley. Off to the left is Wark. You will soon come to a junction, with Heugh to the left. Take the right fork, head to Buteland and left onto the minor road, and so steeply down to Redesmouth.

Battlesteads Hotel

Wark, Hexham, Northumberland NE48 3LS
Run by: Richard Slade

A converted 17th-century farmhouse carefully modernised to provide comfortable and friendly surroundings. Used to cyclists and will help with repairs. New owners pride themselves on superb authentic English cuisine.

- 01434 230 209
- www.battlesteads.com
- info@battlesteads.com
- 4D, 7T, 2F, Disabled 3T and 1D on ground floor
- from £40–£55
- Pk Lunch: £4.75
- Eve Meal: £16.50
- Dist from Reivers: 1 mile (left at Birtley)
- VisitBritain: 4-star inn

The Black Bull

Main St, Wark, Northumberland, NE48 3LG
Run by: Raymond & Sylvia Carr

A 17th century Inn with five en-suite rooms, beer garden, bar restaurant and home cooked food.

- 01434 230239
- www.blackbullwark.co.uk
- info@blackbullwark.co.uk
- 2D, 1T, 2F
- £30–£45
- Eve Meal: Wednesday to Saturday
- Pk Lunch: £5
- Dist from Reivers: 1.5 Miles
- Drying Facilities & Secure Lock-up
- 3 Star Tourist Board, inspected 2007

Bellingham

ABOUT THE VILLAGE

Where Scots and robbers met their match in stone and blood

This ancient little market town (pronounced "Bellinjum") nestles at the foot of some of the wildest and most barren fells in Northumberland. There are medieval references to Bellingham Castle belonging to the King of Scotland's forester, but sadly no trace remains.

St Cuthbert's Church is unusual with its stone roof and extremely narrow windows. Both features were included as a defence against the marauding Scots who twice burnt it to the ground. In its graveyard lies the famous "Lang Pack" grave which is associated with one of Northumberland's most notorious tales of murder, intrigue and deception. One day a peddler (a tinker, not a cyclist) came to Lee Hall, the home of a landed local gentleman and asked if he could leave his backpack there while he attended to an errand in the village. The maid said yes, and it was left in the kitchen.

She noted how big and broad the connicle shaped pack was, but thought no more about it. The gypsy failed to return that day and during the night she came down with a candle and noticed the pack had marginally moved. She ran and fetched old Richards, the wrinkled retainer, who blasted it with a blunderbuss. There followed much blood and whimpering, then silence. Inside was the corpse of a criminal whose dastardly plan was to rob and murder the household in the dead of night. He got more than he bargained for. His grave lies in the churchyard, dated 1723. A plot well foiled!

There is also the St Cuthbert's Well, dedicated to the saint and a welcome addition for thirsty Pennine Way walkers, as it is right next to the pathway for Britain's most famous walk.

On the edge of the Northumberland National Park on the North Tyne river, the Bellingham area is a noted spawning ground for salmon, sea trout, brown trout and the `Kielder' rainbow. It has two caravan sites, a campsite, youth hostel, four pubs and hotels and just about everything else including a haberdashery, gym and library. Also, it is a proper place – not (yet) a haven for second-home owners. The annual agricultural show in the summer (last Saturday in August) is a big attraction with a country fair and Cumberland Westmorland wrestling and Northumbrian piping.

PLACES OF INTEREST

Heritage Centre
Plenty of local history explained, including some excellent background about Reivers, and the Border counties railway which ran from Hexham to Bellingham and across the border. Recreation of old mine workings, plus a shop devoted to the local early 20-centdry photographer WP Collier.
✆ 01434 220050

Hareshaw Linn
Superb waterfall, about 1km walk

St Cuthbert's (Cuddy's) Well
Reputed to be healing water

Tourist Information Centre
Main Street
✆ 01434 220616

BIKE REPAIRS: Village Country Store ✆01434 220027

Riverdale Hall Hotel
Bellingham, Northumberland NE48 2JT
Run by: John Cocker
Country house sporting hotel, with its own swimming pool, sauna, salmon river, cricket field, golf opposite plus all the cycling and walking routes. Real ale in bar. Cocker's 30th year.

✉ reservations@riverdalehallhotel.co.uk
💻 www.riverdalehallhotel.co.uk
✆ 01434 220 254
✆ 01434 220 457
🛏 33 rooms with every conceivable configuration. Ideal for groups.
💷 £36-£49
🍽 Pk Lunch: from £2.60

🍽 Eve Meal: Restaurant from £15, bar £9.
ⓘ 2-star Relais Routier Gold Plate for the restaurant (the only one in Northumberland)

Lyndale Guest House
Riversidewalk, Bellingham, Northumberland NE48 2AW
Run by: Joyce Gaskin
Relax in the sun lounge overlooking the Pennine Way. Look forward to a jacuzzi bath! And tea and biscuits in the garden after a wonderful day out in the countryside.

✆ 01434 220 361
💻 www.lyndaleguest house.co.uk
✉ lyndaleguesthouse@ hotmail.com
🛏 1S, 2D, 1T, 1suite (2 jacuzzi bathrooms)
💷 £30-£45 (single occ of double).

🍽 Pk Lunch: £5
ⓘ Laundry
🍷 Nr pub: 30m
ⓘ 4 star VisitBritain Welcome Host Award

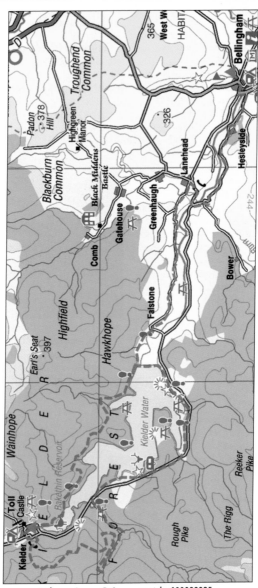

Ordnance Survey © Crown copyright: 100039985

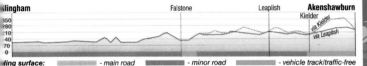

| lingham | | | Falstone | | Leaplish | **Akenshawburn** |

Kielder
via Kielder
via Leaplish

ding surface: ▓▓▓▓ - main road ▓▓▓▓ - minor road ▓▓▓▓ - vehicle track/traffic-free

Falstone

DIRECTIONS

To find the route out of Bellingham follow the signs for Wark and Hexham. Cross the North Tyne, turn right and follow the south bank. You are now in the Northumberland National Park.

Continue for about 7km to the T-junction where you go right back over the Tyne. There follows a climb into Lanehead followed by a left. Close just beyond the remains of Tarset Castle onto the Falstone road.

The secluded little hamlet of Falstone lost nearly 80% of its parish under the waters of Kielder Reservoir. Today the village is a tranquil beauty spot surrounded by trees, and is a good stopping place, with post office, shop and pub.

A tributary to the Tyne bubbles its way through the centre of the village and, depending on the time of year, it is possible to see dippers, heron, cormorants, goosanders, and with luck you may witness the miraculous sight of salmon spawning.

Bellingham–Past Kielder

Most of old Falstone is now covered by the Keilder Reservoir

The Pheasant Inn

Stannersburn, Falstone, NE48 1DD

Run by: Robin Kershaw

Traditional and unspoilt country inn, which features in Alistair Sawday's Special Places to Stay. The food is renowned, as is the beer: game pies, salmon and local lamb as well as wonderful Northumbrian cheeses. Recently refurbished.

- ☏ 01434 240382
- 🖥 www.thepheasantinn.com
- ✉ stay@thepheasantinn.com
- 🛏 4D, 3T, 1F (sleeps 4)
- 💷 £42.50-£50
- 🍴 Eve Meal: 3 courses around £17
- 🍴 Pk Lunch: £7.50
- ⓘ Secure lock up
- 🚲 Dist to Reivers: On route

117

Important choices

**PLEASE READ THE FOLLOWING ROUTE ADVICE CAREFULLY:
IT COULD MAKE OR BREAK YOUR TRIP**

The next stage involves serious route choices which could either make or ruin your holiday. Either way, you take a right turn before the bridge in the centre of Falstone (it is marked as a dead-end), carry on down here for 50m and head left down a track to Hawkhope.

🚲 Your first choice faces you at Hawkhope:

❶ Go left at the junction and head over the dam to join the road.

❷ Take the forestry track along the north shore of Kielder Water. There are Reivers waymarks and also red arrows marked with the figure 6; both lead the same way. The track is good and is 8km in length, until you get to Gowanburn, where a tarmac road hives off to the left, taking you on a wiggly ride to Kielder village. You pass Kielder Castle and its visitor centre before getting to the village.

🚲 Here you have another option:

❸ The sensible one. Take the right turn up past Bell's Burn bridge, Deadwater and Saughtree, then left onto the B6357 and into Newcastleton. This is not the route on the map, but it makes a lot of sense.

❹ Left, then right along Forest Enterprise Route 5c. Be warned, the this path has long, hard climbs.

If you take Option ❶ above, the south shore option at the dam, then do bear in mind that the road can get busy in the summer.

🚲 There is another choice to be faced:

❶ Take the off-road Lewis Burn track to Newcastleton, 3km beyond the Leaplish Water-side Park. This is an extremely arduous off-road section through forestry where even experienced hands have been known to get lost.

❷ Carry on along the aforementioned Saughtree road and head out to Newcastleton along the B6357, keeping your wheels firmly on terra firma.

*NB: I would seriously advise anyone with panniers to take the **ROAD** to Newcastleton, and ignore all suggestions on the Footprint route map trying to lure you into the woods; it is 24km of off-road wilderness, with no services; not even a McDonald's.*

Newcastleton is the only beacon of civilisation (apart from accommodation around Bailey Mill) between Kielder and the village (a seeming metropolis) of Hethersgill, some 30km away.

🚲 If you are fit and unencumbered, there is yet another tough option:

❸ Up Serpent Brae. Go left at the Leaplish centre, under the underpass and beetle up the severe incline before turning right and heading through the forest. You should emerge at somewhere called The Forks, where you join the Lewis Burn route to Akenshawburn, where the track crosses the border and snakes along the Scottish side of the Kershope Burn. At Kershope Bridge you can go right to Newcastleton or turn left towards Bailey Mill and yonder hills.

Kielder

ABOUT THE VILLAGE

Bandit country that has become a haven for wildlife

Nowadays, Kielder Water is a wild and romantic place, but remember it is in the heart of Border Reiver country. It is hard to imagine the cattle rustling, kidnapping and arson that flourished here in the 15th and 16th centuries. Today Kielder's stunning scenery, peace and quiet welcome all visitors.

There is a wealth of facilities for the cyclist here. Northumbria Water, who created the reservoir, has been responsible for a good deal of the inspiration behind the Reivers Cycle Route.

Sadly, the Reivers Rest at the Leaplish Waterside Park has been closed down for the foreseeable future.

Kielder, at the head of the reservoir, was once a wild and uncultivated fastness, where the Border bandits known as Reivers used to roam. It was surrounded by moors and bogs. It is now a purpose-built forestry village cocooned by alpine spruce and pine trees and an oasis for the cyclist with a shop, pub and post office.

The whole area is now far more accessible as multi-purpose tracks have been put in from the dam almost as far as the village, thanks to the Kielder Partnership. This avoids roads which, during the summer, become horribly busy and it is worth the effort of exploring for the variety of wildlife including the red squirrel – half of all the examples in England of that increasingly rare species are reckoned to be in Kielder.

Before the turn of the century Kielder Castle, which stands guard over the village, would have been hidden and alone at the valley head.

It was built in 1775 by the Duke of Northumberland as his hunting lodge. Shooting parties travelled from London on the sleeper and were met at the station by pony and trap. To carry home a bag of 200 brace of grouse and blackcock in a day was not unusual.

Twenty Seven

27 Castle Drive, NE48 1EQ
Run by: Jill Gregg
Cosy former forester's cottage with multi-fuel stove. Jill lives up the road and serves a splendid breakfast at this relaxing bolt hole in Britain's 'remotest' village. Lock-up and laundry room. Happy to rent place out for self-catering for a minimum of three nights.

- ☎ 01434 250366 or 250462
- 🖥 www.staykielder.co.uk
- ✉ jill@staykielder.co.uk
- 🛏 1S, 1T, 2F
- £ from £28
- 🍽 Eve Meal: On request (£8-£10)
- 🍽 Pk Lunch: £4.50

PLACES OF INTEREST

Kielder Castle

Built in 1775 as a hunting lodge for the Duke of Northumberland, the Castle is now the focal point for visitors to the forest. In the castle there are exhibitions about the forest and its wildlife, and a gallery hosting a different artist each month. The grounds include more cycle ways, a maze, playgrounds, a 13-mile forest drive and a bird-viewing platform. Open April to October.

✆ 01434 250209

Leaplish Waterside Park

Heated swimming pool and sauna, campsite, accommodation together with a licensed restaurant, sculpture trail, bird of prey centre, and much more. Open from April - October.

✆ 0870 240 3549

BIKE SHOP

The Bike Place

Rescue service, repairs, accessories and clothing plus a hire service. Big business in a small place. Ian, Justin or Ian.

✆ 01434 250 457

OTHERS

Kielder YHA

Kielder Village, NE48 1HQ
✆ 01434 250195
✉ kielder@yha.org.uk

The Anglers Arms

✆ 01434 250 072

Kielder Ferry Service

80-seater cruiser takes you round the lake — from Tower Knowe to Leaplish to Kielder Castle. Facilities on board include bar, commentary, shop, heated lounge and toilets.

✆ 0870 240 3549

Tower Knowe Visitor Centre

Has an extensive gitt shop and audio-visual exhibition. On south bank very near the dam wall. Open daily 10-4/5. There is a ferry point, souvenir and fishing shop, exhibition centre, picnic area, extensive lavatory facilities, self-guided trails, sailing club and a restaurant

✆ 0870 2403549

Kielder Water Club

Sailing club and yacht club plus a water-ski club. Watercraft hire: range of canoes, kayaks, toppers, wayfarers and dinghies.

✆ 01434 250217

Cycling

Yes, even cycling: apart from the Reivers, there are many different routes which might interest those of you who are doing a detour here, or perhaps meeting up with the family. Get a Cycling at Kielder brochure from Tower Knowe or Leaplish Waterside Park.

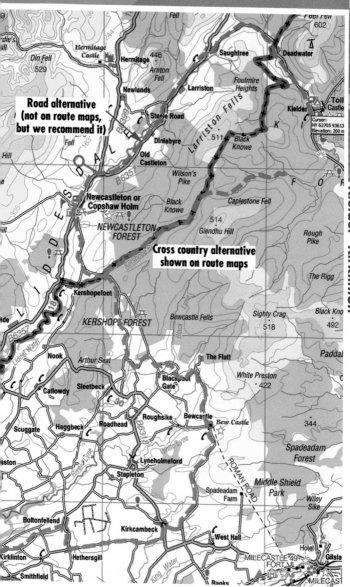

Road alternative (not on route maps, but we recommend it)

Cross country alternative shown on route maps

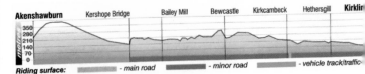

Newcastleton

ABOUT THE VILLAGE

Custom-built with extra large windows for cottage industry

With its broad Georgian streets and open squares, it is no surprise to learn that that Newcastleton was purpose designed and built from scratch by the Duke of Buccleuch (in 1792).

The changes in agriculture meant that there was a need for more village-based employment such as handloom weaving and unusually for the time, the houses were built with large windows to let in light for the new cottage industries.

The town has a post office, several pubs, an antique shop , a bank, a grocery and several guest-houses. Also the garage will help with bike repairs and there is also the interesting Liddesdale Heritage Centre.

If your time and energy allow, then don't miss out on the short detour to Hermitage Castle.

This mysterious and magical place not only witnessed long years of turbulent border reiving, but it played host to the tragic Mary Queen of Scots when she snatched two hours' rendezvous with her lover Bothwell.

Liddesdale Hotel

17 Douglas Sq, Newcastleton, TD9 0QD
Run by: Jamie Carruthers

Newly refurbished family hotel now has a suite, complete with 4-poster. There is a new emphasis on food and the D, B&B at £50 looks good value. Fully licensed with a secure lock-up for bikes. A handsome and solid building sitting in the main square.

- ☏ 013873 75255
- 🖥 www.liddesdalehotel.co.uk
- ✉ reception@liddesdalehotel.co.uk
- 🛏 1S, 2D,2T/F, 1 suite
- 💰 From £30 (£50 D,B&B)
- 🍽 Pk Lunch: On request
- 🍽 New fine dining restaurant. £5-£18.
- 🚲 Dist to Reivers: On route

Woodside

North Hermitage Street, Newcastleton, TD9 0RZ
Run by: Michael Bogg

Red sandstone house built circa 1870 retains many original Victorian features. All rooms are centrally heated and double glazed. Large garden and parking for a dozen cars. En-suite rooms and  secure block-up and washing facilities.

- ☏ 013873 75431
- ✉ woodside@theboggies.e7even.com
- 🛏 1S, 1D, 1T plus self-catering bungalow for six.
- 💰 £22-£25
- 🍽 Pk Lunch: £4
- 🍽 Eve meal: No, but pub nearby
- 🚲 Dist to Reivers : On route
- ⓘ Cycle storage. Wash down facilities

The Grapes Hotel
16 Douglas Square,
Newcastleton,
Roxburghshire, TD9 0QD
Run by: Trevor & Glenys
    Cambridge

Family run hotel with four bars, excellent bar meals and an 'A La Carte' restaurant. Lock-up for bikes and drying facilities. In a lovely spot; lively or restful – it's up to you.

✆ 013873 75245/75680
✆ 013873 75896

🖥 www.the-grapes-hotel.com
📧 info@the-grapes-hotel.com
🛏 1S, 2D, 1T, 1D/F, 1X4S, 1 bunkroom
💰 From £20
🍴 Pk Lunch: £5
🍴 Eve Meal: From £4.50

Sorbietrees
Newcastleton ,
Roxburghshire,
TD9 0TL
Run by: Sandy
    Reynolds

"A warm welcome awaits you at our lovely farmhouse with its spectacular views, log fires, hearty Aga-cooked breakfasts & lift to the local pub for evening meal if required."

✆ 013873 75215
🖥 www.sorbietrees.co.uk

📧 sandy.sorbietrees@btinternet.com
🛏 2D,1T/F
💰 £25–£35
🍴 Pk Lunch: £3.50
🍴 Eve meal: No

🍺 Nr pub: 2 miles (lift provided)
🚲 Dist to Reivers: On route
ⓘ Drying facilties
ⓘ Secure lock up and bike washing facilities
ⓘ VisitScotland Walking/cycling award

Hermitage Castle has a romantic history

Bewcastle

BAILEY MILL

At the southern end of Newcastleton take a left, heading up the hill past Sorbietrees and down to Kershope Bridge, right up the steep hill to the telephone box and onward to Bailey Mill.

Keep your eyes peeled and follow the Route 10 signs towards Bewcastle. You will soon see a handsome cluster of white buildings that looks as if they have been transported straight from the Dordogne region of France and carefully placed in this harsher clime. This is Bailey Mill, an excellent stop off, whether for food and drink or an overnight stay.

Bailey Mill

Bailey, nr Newcastleton, Roxburghshire, TD9 0TR
Run by: Pam Copeland

Jacuzzi, sauna, public bar, restaurant and all-round comfort. A great stopping off point in one of the more remote areas of the Borderlands. Secure storage, a hose to wash them down, plus drying rooms.

✆ 016977 48617
🖥 www.baileycottages-riding-racing.com
📧 pam@baileymill.fsnet.co.uk

🛏 2S, 5D, 5T, 4F
💷 £25-£35
🍽 Pk Lunch: from £4
🍽 Eve Meal: from £10, 2 courses

BEWCASTLE

The famous Bewcastle Cross (right) has survived 1300 years of relentless border weather in St Cuthbert's churchyard.

The church and remains of the castle stand remote and almost alone save for a farmhouse in this forgotten outpost in a great sweep of wild and rugged countryside.

There is a display of interpretative panels nearby in the small Past & Present Heritage Centre. They tell the story of the Anglo-Saxon cross. The runic inscriptions and carving are of a very high quality for this period in history.

Hethersgill

DIRECTIONS

The stretch to Kircambeck is fairly straight-forward. After that continue to Hethersgill by heading right at Askerton Castle, then left onto the B6318 and first right at Knorren Lodge.

There is not lot deal here, it's a place whose economy has traditionally been fuelled by peat extraction. You can stop for a pint at the Black Lion pub, which belongs to the same folk who run the Drove Inn at nearby Stapleton.

There are various accommodation choices at places such as Walton and Stapleton – none of them exactly on the route, but all worth a stopover to get a real flavour of the area.

Two possibilities are Low Luckens and New Pallyards. To reach either, take the route past Hethersgill up to Boltonfellend. Instead of turning left on the signposted route, head straight on, bearing left at the junction with the

"Summer is for grazing, but autumn is for raiding"

The Reivers were far too busy tending crops and fattening the cattle in summer to be doing any plundering, but as soon as the crops were gathered and the horses fit they would be hot foot across the border to get down to the serious winter business of stealing each other's wives, girl-friends, cattle, sheep and carefully-stored winter goods again.

main road. Continue across the river, taking the second left for New Pallyards, or first right for Low Luckens. If opting for the latter, take a further right after 500m, opposite a farm a kilometre or so up the road; follow a metalled road up to Low Luckens. This delightful backwater is called Roweltown.

Kielder–Kirklinton

Low Luckens Organic Resource Centre

Roweltown, nr.Hethersgill, Carlisle, CA6 6LJ.
Run by: Jill Jones

Self-catering hostel-type accommodation on an organic farm. Supplies, including organic produce, sometimes available if ordered in advance. Four miles NNE of Hethersgill grid ref NY494726 (OS Sheet 86)."

- 016977 48186
- lowluckensorc@hotmail.com
- www.lowluckensfarm.co.uk
- 1S, 2F/group
- Self catering: £12-£15
- Dist to Reivers : 4.5km nr Roadhead (Stapleton on the Reivers map).
- Nr Pub: 6km

New Pallyards

Hethersgill, Nr Carlisle, Cumbria CA6 6HZ
Run by: Georgina and John Elwen

"Farmhouse accommodation & self catering cottages. Residential licence, cycles undercover, large groups welcome. National Gold Award."

- 01228 577308
- www.4starsc.co.uk
- newpallyards@btinternet.com
- £30-£35
- 2S, 2D, 3T, 2F + self-catering units
- Pk Lunch: £4.50
- Eve Meal: £16 (set menu)
- Dist to Reivers: 3km
- Nr Pub: on site

From Hethersgill follow signs to Boltonfellend and head left to Kirklinton. You are on the river Lyne, not far from Longtown. There are lots of tiny communities around here.

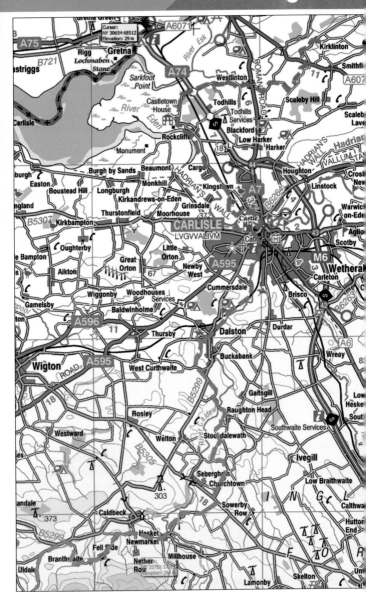

Ordnance Survey © Crown copyright: 100039985

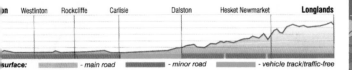
surface: ▓▓▓ - main road ▓▓▓ - minor road ▓▓▓ - vehicle track/traffic-free

Westlinton / Longtown

ABOUT THE VILLAGE

Reiving centre that found respectability

This area which looks so cultivated and prosperous (putting aside the wretched chapter of foot and mouth in 2001) was once so violent that it was only 300 years ago that there was any proper settlement outside Carlisle. The handsome bastion on Longtown's high street, the Graham Hotel, bears the name of the family who settled the town.

They were also among the most infamous of the reiving families (see p.102) and are one of the reasons there are some 90 pele towers (see picture) scattered around this area – the only way of staying alive and keeping your cattle was to put them behind a thick stone wall when the riders were abroad.

With respectability came not only the Graham Hotel, but high street banks, so if you are running low there are a couple of cash dispensers there.

To reach Longtown, turn right and head up the A6071 for 3km just beyond Kirklinton, or cross the A7 and turn right a few hundred metres past the Lynebank House Hotel. This takes you onto the Route 7 cycle way, the Lochs & Glens route linking Carlisle and Glasgow.

Kirklinton–Longlands

Lynebank Guest House

Westlinton, nr Carlisle, Cumbria CA6 6AA
Run by: Duncan Todhunter

17th century coaching house recently renovated to nine-bedroom hotel, restaurant and bar. All rooms en suite. Licensed. Secure cycle parking in landscaped courtyard. Kannyble's restaurant has vegetarian options. Free pint for the first person to guess the provenance of the restaurant name.

- 01228 792 820
- 01228 792 816
- www.lynebank.co.uk
- info@lynebank.co.uk
- 3S, 3D, 2T, 1F
- £22.50–£40 (with a bridal suite option)
- Pk Lunch: from £4.50
- Eve Meal: £5.85–£29.50
- Dist to Reivers: On route
- VisitBritain: 4 stars

127

Carlisle

DIRECTIONS

The route from Westlinton to the city takes you down to the edge of the Solway Firth, where the rivers Eden and Esk meet and swell a progress across vast acres of mud and sand until disgorging into the Irish Sea beyond Bowness and Annan.

Here you pass such erstwhile centres of shipbuilding as Rockliffe and other vestiges of a prosperous past, before cutting through a large and unattractive industrial estate. Soon, however, you are in the heart of a vibrant and welcoming city. You cross the River Eden at the bridge by the Sands centre, turn right and pedal past the front of the impressive castle before crossing the main road, swinging left down Viaduct Estate Road and out of town alongside the River Caldew.

These days this great border city greets its guests with open arms, but not so many years ago any visitor would have been treated with suspicion. It was the nerve-centre for bitter feuds and bloody battles created by the long-running dispute over the border between England and Scotland. Early in its history it was an important Roman headquarters for Hadrian's Wall. In 1092 William the

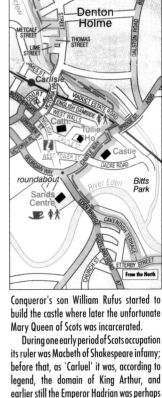

Conqueror's son William Rufus started to build the castle where later the unfortunate Mary Queen of Scots was incarcerated.

During one early period of Scots occupation its ruler was Macbeth of Shakespeare infamy; before that, as `Carluel' it was, according to legend, the domain of King Arthur, and earlier still the Emperor Hadrian was perhaps the first to realise that whoever held Carlisle was in the perfect position to influence the destinies of both England and Scotland.

PLACES OF INTEREST

Carlisle Castle
You only have to look at the vast ramparts of the castle to realise the city's strategic importance. It is the home today of the King's Own Border Regiment. If you get time, it is worth looking at its labyrinths to find the Licking Stones, prisoners carvings and the exhibition of Bonnie Prince Charlie's capture of the castle in 1745.
(01228 591922

Carlisle Cathedral
Founded in 1122, fine wood carving and wall panels
(01228 548151 (office)

EATING

Number 10
Eden Mount
Probably Carlisle's best eaterie. Small, popular and on route, so book well in advance.
(01228 524183

Almonds Bistro
Angus Hotel
Great fun, good food and reasonably priced.
(01228 523546

Loaf `n Ladle
16 Friars Court
Value for money vegetarian food.
(01228 596474

Tullie House Museum & Art Gallery
Excellent audio-visual interpretation of the Border Reivers.
(01228 534781

Around the town
Carlisle's cultural renaissance and growing reputation for education have resulted in a host of art galleries, restaurants, cafés and vibey venues. The city's long-running commercial success is celebrated in the Guildhall Museum, once a meeting place of the medieval trade guilds.

Queen Victoria still rules over Bitt Park in Carlisle

CYCLE SHOPS

Palace Cycle Stores
122 Botchergate
(01228 523142

Scotby Cycles
Old Bingo Hall, Church Street
(01228 546931

Abberley House
33 Victoria Place, Carlisle, CA1 1HP
Run by: G Shipp

City centre guest house, offering good quality en-suite rooms, secure lock-up and drying facilities. Close to restaurants, pubs and shops. Prices include a full English breakfast.

- ☎ 01228 521 645
- 🖥 www.abberleyhouse.co.uk
- ✉ enquiries@abberleyhouse.co.uk
- 🛏 3S, 2D, 2T, 1F.
- 💷 £25-£30
- ⓘ 4 stars
- 🍺 Nr pub: 300m

White Lea Guest House
191 Warwick Road, Carlisle CA1 1LP
Run by: Gillian Denison

Victorian town house right in the town centre with all its facilities. All rooms en-suite with TV, hairdryer and welcome tray. Fully refurbished and immaculate throughout, there's also private parking.

- ☎ 01228 533 139
- 🖥 www.whiteleacarlisle.co.uk
- 🛏 1D, 1T, 2F.
- 💷 £25-£30.
- 🍴 Pk Lunch: £4.50
- 🚲 Dist to Reivers: 1km.
- ⓘ VisitBritain 4 stars
- 🍺 Nr pub: 100m

Langleigh Guest House
6 Howard Place, Carlisle, CA1 1HR
Run by: Yvette Rogers

Highly recommended by many tourists organisations. Private road parking, five minutes from city centre, welcome trays, spacious rooms. Ideal resting place before the last stage.

- ☎ 01228 530 440
- 🖥 www.langleighhouse.co.uk
- ✉ langleighhouse@aol.com
- 🛏 1S + 3D + 3T + 1F
- 💷 £35
- 🍴 Pk Lunch: £5
- 🍴 Eve Meal: £10-£25
- ⓘ 4 stars
- 🍺 Nr pub: 5 minutes
- ⓘ Lock-up/drying facilities

Kenilworth Guest House
34 Lazonby Terrace, CA1 2PZ
Run by: Robert & Anne Glendinning

Family business. Friendly, warm welcome. Big Cumbrian breakfast or something lighter if required. Edwardian town

house with comfortable en-suite rooms and open fires.
- ☎ 01228 526 179
- ✉ reception@kenilworth-guesthouse.co.uk
- 🖥 www.kenilworth-guesthouse.co.uk
- 🛏 1S, 2D, 1T, 1F (E-S).
- 💷 £25-£30
- 🍴 Pk Lunch: £4
- 🚲 Dist to Reivers: 1km
- 🍺 Nr pub 100m

Derwentlea

14 Howard Place, CA1 1HR
Run by: Yvette Rogers

A warm Victorian house in a quiet conservation area with private car park and only five minutes walk from the city centre. Family rooms, cots, highchairs available; drying facilities; laundry service; secure lockable storage. All rooms are en-suite and have tea and coffee making facilities and colour TVs.

* 01228 409706
  07970 209760
  www.derwentlea.co.uk

  general@derwentlea.co.uk
  2S, 5T/D
  £35
  Eve Meal: £10-£25 (BYOB)
  Pk Lunch: £5
  i Drying facilities. Safe storage

Hazeldean Guest House

Orton Grange, Wigton Road, Carlisle, Cumbrian CA5 6JB
Run by: Susan Harper

Friendly guest house, 50m from Reivers route. Large garden, secure parking for bikes. Complimentary therapies available—massage, reflexology and reiki. Spa suite, hot tub and sauna.

* 01228 711 953
  www.hazeldean
    therapycentre.com
  hazeldean1@
    btopenworld.com
  1S, 2D, 1T (SP: lounge)
  £26
  Pk Lunch: from £3.50
  Eve Meal: £7-£10.
  Dist to Reivers: On route
  i VisitBritain 3 stars
  Pub nearby

Courtfield Guest House

169 Warwick Road, Carlisle CA1 1LP
Run by: Marjorie Dawes

Comfortable, en-suite bedrooms, TV, tea/coffee facilities. Ten minute walk to historic Carlisle city centre. Rightly famed for its breakfast – a classy fry or fruit and yoghurt style options. Cycle friendly and very well run.

* 01228 522 767
  £27.50-£30

  mdawes@
    courtfieldhouse.
    fsnet.co.uk
  1S, 3D, 2T, 2F.
  Pk Lunch: £5
  i VisitBritain 4 stars/
    Silver Award
  Nr pub: 200m

Angus Hotel & Almonds Bistro

14 Scotland Road, Carlisle CA3 9DG
Run by: Martin & Rachel Perry

Small family run hotel offering personal hospitality, and superb food in Almonds Restaurant. Licensed bar, secure cycle store, drying facilities, packed lunches. Groups welcome.

* 01228 523 546

* 01228 531 895
  www.angus-hotel.co.uk
  hotel@angus-
    hotel.co.uk
  2S, 5D, 4T, 3F.
  £28-£50.
  Pk Lunch: £4.70
  Eve Meal: £15
    (3-courses)
  Dist to Reivers: On route

Aaron House
135 Warwick Road,
Carlisle, CA1 1LU.
Run by: Blanche Tiffin

Family run B&B, centrally heated, en-suite facilities available, TV and welcome tray in rooms, special diets by prior arrangement.

- ✆ 01228 536 728
- 🛏 1T, 2F
- 💷 £25-£30
- 🍽 Pk Lunch: £4
- 🚲 Dist to Reivers: 1km

Ashleigh House
46 Victoria Place, Carlisle, CA1 1EX
Run by: Alan Dawes

Just yards from the cycle route, there's a warm welcome in this family run Grade II listed Victorian town house, two minutes' walk from the city centre. All bedrooms en-suite with tea and coffee making facilities. For those staying longer or returning, there's golf, fishing and wonderful walking.

- ✆ 01228 521631
- 🛏 1S, 2D, 2T, 1F, 2Tpl.
- 💷 £30-£35
- ℹ VisitBritain 4 stars
- 🍺 Nr pub: 200m
- ℹ Drying facitlities. Secure lock-up

Greysteads Private Hotel
43 Norfolk Rd, Carlisle CA2 5PQ
Run by: Michael Potts

Elegant and old fashioned family run hotel in a quiet part of town yet within easy reach of the centre. Bedrooms all offer tea and coffee facilities plus TV and there's bags of parking space and a large secure lock-up area. Greysteads is on the way out of town heading south, towards the Dalston road and is right next to the route. Afternoon teas available.

- ✆ 01228 522175
- ✉ michael.potts@greysteads.co.uk

- 🛏 2T, 2D, 1S.
- 💷 from £25
- 🍽 Pk Lunch: From £4

Hesket Newmarket

THE VILLAGE

Ask a local the name of an ash tree and he will tell you it is a `hesh'. Hesket means the place of the ash tree. It is a pleasant village that invites travellers to rest, featuring a medieval stone stall that was used until the late 1900s to tether bulls for the local cattle market. There is a well-stocked village shop, a post office, a couple of guest houses and the Old Crown Inn with its increasingly well-known microbrewery.

You are in the Eastern Fells of the Lake District National Park, a miraculously untouched corner of England that proved a magnet for St Mungo in the 6th century, when he came, saw and converted. Many local churches are dedicated to him, usually under his real name: Kentigern (Mungo is a nickname meaning "dear friend").

You are about to tackle the toughest bit of the ride with some challenging up-and-down and majestic views. To the south west you will see the Lake District opening up, with great views of Skiddaw and the Uldale Fells.

Denton House

Hesket Newmarket, nr Caldbeck, Cumbria CA7 8JG
Run by: Susan Armstrong

Friendly atmosphere with home cooking and log fires awaits you in this modernised 17th century house. En-suite rooms with tea/coffee making facilities. Lock-up for bikes.

- 016974 78415
- dentonhnm@aol.com
- www.dentonhouseguesthouse.co.uk
- 2D, 3T, 3F.
- £26-£30
- Pk Lunch: £5
- Dist to Reivers: On route

- Pub nearby (with own brewery)
- 4 stars
- Lock-up/drying facilities.

Greenhill Farm

Hesket Newmarket, CA 7 8JG.
Run by: Arthur & Joan Todhunter

Splendid little campsite on a working farm near the edge of the village, 250 yards from the brewery and pub/restaurant.

- 016974 78453

Newlands Grange

Hesket-Newmarket, nr Wigton, Cumbria CA7 8HP
Run by: Mrs Dorothy Studholme

Newlands Grange is a working farm looking onto the Caldbeck Fells. The house features old oak beams and open fire. Good home-cooking and a warm welcome awaits all. Transport to the local pub

- 016974 78676
- studholme_newlands@hotmail.com
- 1S, 2D, 2T/F (E-S)
- £24-£26.50
- Pk Lunch: £4
- Eve Meal: £10
- Dist to Reivers: On route
- Nr pub: 1 mile

Caldbeck

ABOUT THE VILLAGE

When water powered the wheels of industry

Named after the river (Cold-beck), Caldbeck was a thriving rural industrial centre long before steam-power and the Industrial Revolution.

In 1800 there were no fewer than eight water-powered mills making bobbins, woollens and grinding corn.

The Priests Mill which has been beautifully restored houses a craft centre, display area and restaurant with a picture gallery. There is even a clog-maker still to be found in the village centre.

In the churchyard, pictured above, is grave of John Peel, the famous Cumbrian Huntsman, and that of Mary, the Beauty of Buttermere who was the subject of the novel 'The Maid of Buttermere' by Melvyn Bragg.

Lord Bragg, incidentally, hails from nearby Wigton and is understandably proud of his local routes (he's a keen cyclist).

PLACES TO EAT

Priests Mill
Delicious vegetarian food

Odd Fellows Arms
Pub food and accommodation

PLACES OF INTEREST

The Howk
Beautiful hidden pathway through the woods to a waterfall and the aforementioned mill. Take a break and have a look...

The Clog Maker
Will Strong: Next to the bridge.

Ireby & Longlands
DIRECTIONS & WATERING HOLES

Arguably the best scenery on the entire round trip

After Caldbeck, the route winds its way round the fell, an area known locally as Back `a Skiddaw, for obvious reasons. If you have done the C2C route, then you will have seen the Front `a Skiddaw.

The Parkend Restaurant and the Snooty Fox at Uldare are two notable watering holes in this mainly empty stretch of untamed wilderness.

This is gloriously open and unspoilt countryside with few stopping places apart from Ireby, just a couple of miles up the road. To get to Ireby, simply continue down the B5299 instead of taking the track to Baggra Yeat.

To get back onto the route, simply continue through the village (ignore the right turn to High Ireby) and you get back on track just beyond Ruthwaite.

In my view, this section is as good as anywhere on the entire C2C & Reivers route. Pointed peaks emerge from the rolling flow of hills, juxtaposing dark shadows with patches of brilliant sunshine in the autumn afternoon I was last on the route.

There are still a couple of serious up-and-downs to come. Take your time — indeed, you will have to courtesy of the topography — through Fellside, Branthwaite and Longlands.

Woodlands Country House Hotel
CA7 1EX
Run by: Judith Wills & Stephen Ort

This beautiful former parsonage has some stunning views and is in the heart of an unspoilt section of the Northern Lakes. Part of the VisitBritain Cyclists Welcome scheme, it is fully licensed and does a splendid 4-course dinner with coffee. A great place for the last night.

- ☎ 016973 71791
- 💷 £32-£43

- 🖥 www.woodlandsatireby.co.uk
- ✉ stay@woodlandsatireby.co.uk
- 🛏 7D/T–3 of which will convert to Triples
- 🍴 Eve Meal: £22 for hearty 4 course dinner plus coffee
- ⓘ VisitBritain 4 stars
- 🍷 Fully licensed

Whitefield Cottage
Overwater, Nr Ireby, Cumbria CA7 1HH.
Run by: Ron & Heike Howes

Superbly and stylishly restored house on the edge of the Caldbeck Fells with stunning views across the back of Skiddaw. Set in four acres of landscaped gardens, Ron is a British canoeing coach and outdoor activities instructor, fisherman and organiser. Plenty of bike storage space.

- ☎ 017687 76357
- 🖥 www.whitefieldcottage.co.uk
- ✉ info@whitehfieldcottage.co.uk

- 💷 £30-£50
- 🛏 1D, 2T.
- 🍴 Eve Meal: Lifts provided to pubs or restaurants within 5 mile radius
- ⓘ Storage. Plenty of parking space

135

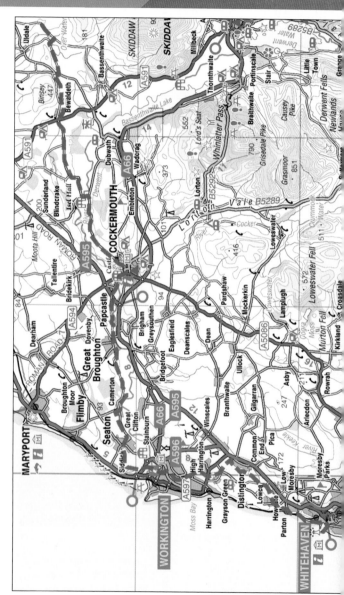

Ordnance Survey © Crown copyright: 100039985

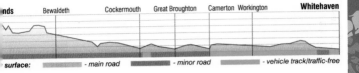

| nds | Bewaldeth | Cockermouth | Great Broughton | Camerton | Workington | **Whitehaven** |

surface: ▬▬▬▬ - main road   ▬▬▬▬ - minor road   ▬▬▬▬ - vehicle track/traffic-free

DIRECTIONS

There are some steep bits as you emerge from Longlands, but once you get to Bewaldeth it is fairly easy riding into Cockermouth, a delightful stop-off for those who fancy a leisurely finish.

When you have crossed the A591, just beyond Bewaldeth, continue along the lane until you get to the crossroads, where you turn left to cross the River Derwent before heading right at the next crossroads.

Once you have passed Hewthwaite Hall (on the right) it is plain sailing into Cockermouth, where you arrive perilously close to the Jennings brewery.

Those who can avoid such temptations might wish to push on to Workington or Whitehave, the official finishing point. However, I find Cockermouth quite irrestible – fine ales, great fish and chips and one of the best vegetarian restaurants in Britain (the Quince & Medlar).

One could quite easily undo all the benefits of several days hard cycling amongst such temptations.

You pass Bassenthwaite and the nearby hills

Longlands – Whitehaven

137

Cockermouth

Full details in the C2C section of the guide: Pages 28 – 30

DIRECTIONS

The route through Cockermouth differs from the C2C only in that you are heading from north to south, instead of vice versa (the detail map, right, has north at the bottom and south at the top).

You arrive near Jennings Brewery and head up Main Street, passing the Tourist Information and Toy Museum before taking a sharp right and heading towards Popcastle.

There are plenty of things to do and lots of excellent places to eat and drink, which are covered in detail in the C2C section of this guide.

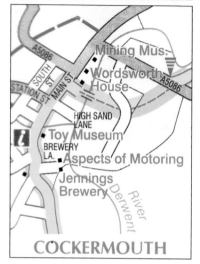

PLACES TO STAY

Try these B&Bs: Full details in C2C section, Page 30

Allerdale Court Hotel, *Market Place, CA13 9NQ*
☏ 01900 823654

Rose Cottage, *Lorton Road, Cockermouth, Cumbria CA13 9DX*
☏ 01900 822189

Riverside, *12 Market St, Cumbria, CA13 9NJ*
☏ 01900 827504

There's spectacular scenery on the approach to Cockermouth

Workington

Full details in the C2C section of the guide: Pages 24 – 27

DIRECTIONS

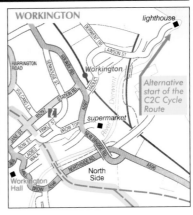

The road from Cockermouth to Workington follows the course of the Derwent via Papcastle, following the C2C in reverse, with the river on your left.

About 4km beyond Great Broughton is Camerton. At the Black Tom climb up to the right and at the old stone bridge hang a left onto the cycle track that takes you to Workington via Seaton.

Again, be warned the map, right, shows the route coming in from the north, which is at the bottom.

Try these B&Bs: Full details in C2C section, Page 27

PLACES TO STAY

Morven House Hotel
Siddick Road, Workington, Cumbria CA14 1LE
℡ 01900 602118

Armidale Cottages
29 High Seaton, CA14 1PD
℡ 01900 63704

Longlands–Whitehaven

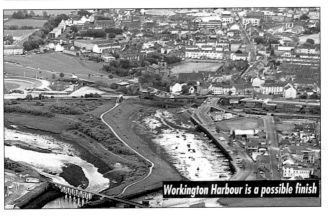

Workington Harbour is a possible finish

Whitehaven

Full details in the C2C section of the guide: Pages 13 – 16

DIRECTIONS
Homeward bound

The final stretch is pretty straightforward. You head out of Workington to Distington where you head for the coast, reaching it at the old Roman fort at Parton Bay and on to Whitehaven. Don't forget to dip your wheel in the briny.

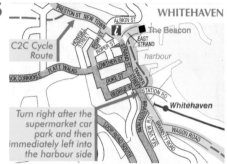

C2C Cycle Route

WHITEHAVEN

The Beacon

harbour

Whitehaven

Turn right after the supermarket car park and then immediately left into the harbour side

---

Try these B&Bs: Full details in C2C section, Page 16

PLACES TO STAY

Waverley Hotel
Tangier St, CA28 7UX
☏ 01946 694337

The Mansion
Old Woodhouse, Whitehaven, Cumbria CA28 9LN
☏ 01946 61860

Glenfield Guest House
Whitehaven, Cumbria, CA28 7TS
☏ 01946 691911

The Marina at Whitehaven harbour: journey's end

JUBILEE ADVENTURE CENTRE

Set in the beautiful village of Crawleyside, Weardale, County Durham

COFFEE AND SNACKS

NADINE KIPLING: 01388 763712

SLEEPING ACCOMMODATION FOR 42 – £3.50 A NIG

SHOWERS AND FULL FACILITIES

WELL EQUIPPED KITCHEN AND DINING ROOM,

INCLUDES CROCKERY